Bud Smith
With Bill Slivka

Hands-On Consulting
As a Framework for Solving Business Problems

Third Edition

Pearson Learning Solutions, 330 Hudson Street, New York, New York 10013
A Pearson Education Company
www.pearsoned.com

Printed in the United States of America

1 2 3 4 5 6 7 8 9 10 v092 18 17 16 15

000200010272013225

JHA/KS

ISBN 10: 1-323-30545-9
ISBN 13: 978-1-323-30545-4

Contents

Acknowledgements

I wish to recognize the contributions of a few individuals. Bill Slivka, Executive-in-Residence at the Katz Graduate School of Business, contributed significantly in developing the text and provided me with a supportive sounding board.

Outside of the University of Pittsburgh, Joe Bozada (former Deloitte consultant) and Dr. Eric Paljug (former McKinsey consultant) were particularly insightful in suggesting how best to deliver the book's message.

I am further indebted to Warren Bennis, then-Professor at the MIT Sloan School of Management, who introduced me to team dynamics and organization leadership. I also acknowledge Howard Caterson, Frank Haas, and John Chrisman of Booz-Allen & Hamilton, for passing along aggressive interviewing techniques and their tough-minded approach to turning data into actionable recommendations.

My wife Carolyn has been particularly supportive throughout this time-consuming undertaking.

George M. (Bud) Smith, Jr.
Pittsburgh, Pennsylvania
September, 2015

Introduction

Ben Franklin had it right:

> "Experience is the best teacher,
> but only fools learn
> from no other"[1]

Building on Dr. Franklin's observation, the author believes that, through the eyes of novice consultants, client engagements can appear uncontrollable, like Franklin's electrical storm deciding where lightning should strike.

Consulting engagements can be like that. True, some client engagements progress smoothly with the issue clear and consistent, the needed data at hand, all client stakeholders on the same page, and a follow-up client engagement lined up. But more often than not, stormy weather follows when client confusion, ambiguity or indifference is in the air.

So the question is: how can novice consultants prepare themselves to handle any and all client engagements? How can he or she improve chances for success? This book addresses such questions. Moreover, the book's premise is that novice consultants' success can be facilitated by applying a framework to resolve client problems or issues, and doing so in an effective and professional manner.

First, however, some instructive observations are necessary. In the pages below, "consultant" refers to business consultants who address general business problems or issues. Excluded are professionals addressing only part of the client's problem, such as auditors, attorneys, employment recruiters, web designers, and so on. Individuals or firms promoting pre-packaged solutions are also excluded, as are individuals retained as implement agents. Management consultants are included as consultants, these individuals viewed as a sub-set of business consulting.

Clients need also to be characterized. A client will engage a consultant to somehow improve the performance of its business or organization. Clients may be business, governmental, or non-profit organizations; they may be large or small. From the client's view-  point, consultants are retained for a variety of reasons. The client may lack problem-solving skills within its organization. Or, the client seeks an outsider's view, free from the preconceptions and the vested interests of client management. Or, an urgent situation may arise the organization lacking anyone available to address the situation in the timeframe required. Other reasons exist for hiring consultants, such as wanting the consultant's help in implementing an earlier recommendation. The resulting client–consultant relationship is referred to as an "engagement."

Engagements unavoidably involve ambiguity. Ambiguity stems from a number of sources. The client may lack the resources to solve its problems: never enough time, never enough money. Some clients have difficulty in defining their problems, while other clients cannot come to grips with differing goals among their managers. In the client's view, the consultant is paid to untangle these ambiguities.

Another source of ambiguity is a tendency among clients to "silo" their problems. Chronic business problems – be these marketing, finance, manufacturing, supply chain, or leadership - rarely reside in a single silo. More often, the client's issues reach across organization lines. For example: while the client may for represent its problem as one embedded in the business's marketing department, the consultant may find that the problem actually stem from poor packaging, late deliveries, or from inefficiencies found elsewhere in the organization.

Additionally, consultants find that clients may not understand their own problems. Rather, consultants end up navigating through a potpourri of symptoms, side issues, and conflicting viewpoints. In order to develop workable solutions, the consultant may have to take the lead in sorting this out.

Ambiguity also enters when the client believes it needs the best solution. As experienced consultants recognize, implementing the best solution takes time, more time than the client may be willing to pay for. Moreover, one client's executive's definition of "best" may conflict with that of another. From a practical standpoint, the client rarely needs "best," but instead requires solutions that are workable and straightforward in their implementation. To reduce ambiguity, consultants find themselves helping the client navigate the murky waters between "best" and "practicable".

Experienced consultants therefore expect ambiguity. They recog-nize it, weight its relevancy, and find ways to move through it. Dealing successfully with client ambiguity is key to the consultant's success because, at the end of the day, clients want their issue resolved within budget, on time and with an acceptable solution sold to client stakeholders. The consultant is responsible for making this happen.

Hands-On Consulting sets out to provide a framework and methods to help the novice consultant find workable solutions and recommendations. In doing so the book first traces the roots of management consulting, and those individuals and consulting firms that built the profession as it is today. Thereafter, the book focuses on what consultants do—how they initiate client engagements, apply problem-solving methods, and add value to their clients.

The book will be helpful to two different but related practitioners. First and foremost is the novice professional consultant. The other are fledging executives. This second group of men and women will come to realize that the business consulting framework mirrors competencies required of senior executives in directing their organizations: gaining consensus, drawing on the right information, managing time and resource....skills shared by senior executives and experienced consultants alike. Recognizing this, the framework set forth in Hands-On Consulting draws on the experience of the many consultants and executives who have over the years contributed to the practice of business consulting.

Roots of Business Consulting

As a profession, business consulting took time to develop.[1] The profession's roots reach back into the nineteenth century. Since then, the profession's myriad frameworks, approaches and methods have evolved and been shaped by its many firms and practitioners. This chapter explores those roots, progress made in building the profession, and challenges faced by professional business consultants and their firms.

The profession of business consulting traces back to **Frederick W. Taylor**. In 1893, while working out of his Philadelphia home, Taylor figured out that factories would pay him to improve worker efficiency. Advising managers of America's fledgling steel industry, Taylor developed what he called "scientific management," a process he defined as follows:

- Studying the work and developing efficient methods to get the job done, Taylor introduced time-study and other methods to calculate work pace.

- Hiring and training workers based on the factory's needs and dismissing the practice of leaving employee development to chance.

- Providing workers with on-the-job instruction.

- Focusing managers on supervision and work planning, leaving the actual work to workers.

To many, Taylor's methods were radical, even revolutionary. Plant operators, however, saw value in his thinking. As the twentieth century began, Taylor's scientific method gained traction. His methods contributed significantly to the vast fortunes acquired by steel entrepreneurs such as Andrew Carnegie.

Arthur D Little About the same time that Taylor was developing his scientific method, Arthur D. Little began putting together a different kind of consulting practice. Little was an MIT-trained chemist. His idea was to perform chemical research, not as a university employee but as a professional working for a fee.[2] By 1909, Little's practice had advanced sufficiently for Little to create the Boston-based consulting firm of **Arthur D Little** or ADL.

ADL's early work included refining papermaking processes and surveying Canada's natural resources. During World War II, ADL developed for the U.S. government a process for converting seawater into drinkable water.

By the 1950s, ADL was applying its methods to management issues. Drawing on probability methods developed for wartime use, ADL became a pioneer in applying quantitative analyses to what later became known as supply chain management. ADL was among the first to apply operations research to management problems. ADL also applied its methods to developing the economy of Puerto

Rico, streamlining European telecom, and privatizing the British Rail system. ADL prides itself as being the world's oldest management consultancy. The firm continues to link client strategy, technology and innovation into deliverable results.[3]

Meanwhile, in Chicago, two additional business consulting firms evolved, differing in style but both becoming consulting powerhouses.

Of the two, **Booz, Allen & Hamilton**, or BA&H came first. In 1914, Edwin Booz left Northwestern University

Booz | Allen | Hamilton

with a degree in Psychology. Despite his limited business experience, Booz noticed that local companies recruited and paid impartial experts to attack their problems. Acting on his insight, Booz attracted his first major client, the Illinois State Railroad. Booz soon thereafter took in partners George Fry, James Allen and Carl Hamilton. The business consulting firm of BA&H resulted.

World War II provided BA&H with an opportunity to consult with the U.S. military. During the early 1940s, it served as a consultant to the Navy. Although government business proved lucrative, George Fry was uncomfortable with BA&H relying so heavily on government contracts. As a result, Fry departed from the company and formed his own firm, Fry Consultants. BA&H went on to build two practices: government and business consulting. The firm's government practice continued its reliance on clients in Washington. On the business side, BA&H looked first nationally and then globally, attracting a range of clients big and small. Its Chicago base expanded to offices in New York, Cleveland, Detroit, Los Angeles, and then internationally.

During the 1950s, the firm added product life cycle methodology to its practice. Supply chain consulting followed during the 1980s. In 1996, BA&H turned client-centric, targeting selected clients and supporting them with a breadth of strategy that included organizational, operational, and informational technology capabilities.[4] As the 20th century closed, Time Magazine recognized BA&H as the world's largest and most prestigious consulting firm.[5]

McKinsey & Company

The other Chicago consulting firm, **McKinsey & Company**, developed along different lines. Unlike BA&H, McKinsey evolved from a public accounting and legal background. The firm's founder, James McKinsey, began his career as an accounting professor at the University of Chicago. In 1926, he formed McKinsey & Company. Soon after, Tom Kearney joined the firm. From its outset, McKinsey & Company offered both accounting and management engineering services. Its first major client was Chicago's Marshall Field Department Store.

While James McKinsey founded McKinsey, it was Marvin Bower who shaped the firm.[6] In 1933, McKinsey & Company recruited Bower from the prestigious law firm of Jones, Day. Bower brought to McKinsey's 15-man firm a refined sense of professionalism, building on his years as a lawyer. He soon convinced James McKinsey to focus on the management needs of chief executive officers (CEOs), divesting the firm's accounting practice in the process. Tom Kearney saw things differently from Bower, splitting off in 1939 to form A.T. Kearney & Company.

McKinsey thereupon built its reputation on Marvin Bower's idea of catering to client CEOs. Under Bower's leadership, McKinsey sought client engagements that addressed senior management issues: corporate strategy, complex organization, and multi-plant operations. It was Marvin Bower who coined the term "management consulting" and applied it to McKinsey's consulting practice.

The 1950s and 60s were heady times for the then-leading firms of ADL, BA&H, and McKinsey. During these post-WWII years, the country's massive military supply machine was dismantled. As a result, America's factories converted to supplying consumer demand. It didn't take long for General Motors, Ford, and Chrysler to rip out their tank and bomber production lines, and make room for the production of fin-tailed automobiles. Arms producers likewise retooled into pots and pans, and chemical plants shifted from gunpowder to household detergents.

With this rise in consumerism, American business saw huge opportunities to generate growth and profitability. Foreign investments moved ahead on a massive scale; well-capitalized makers of machinery, chemicals, food products, and metal fabricators of all sorts set out for Europe and elsewhere, exploiting their war-advanced production techniques.[7]

The acceptability of using business consultants also evolved. Before WW II, many executives equated hiring a business consultant to admitting to poor corporate health. After the war however, attitudes changed. During the Truman, Eisenhower, and Kennedy years, businesses confronted issues of scale and capital allocation. Moreover, management was forced to deal with organized labor, and to anticipate market opportunity and competitive inroads. Recognizing they were ill equipped to deal with so many issues at the same time, business managers of all stripes sought outside help.

The major consulting firms stepped in. They not only expanded, but experimented with new approaches. BA&H and McKinsey, for example, began recruiting high-potential MBA graduates from Harvard, Stanford, and other influential business schools to handle data collection and analysis—and spend weeks on the road in doing so. BA&H further extended its consulting practice to include industrial engineering and executive search. McKinsey meanwhile levered its organizational capabilities to go global, first with the Shell Group in Venezuela, and then with European clients unable to find such consulting talent locally.[8] America's consulting industry was enjoying a period of growth and success.

 But no one expected OPEC. In 1973, Arab members of the Organization of Petroleum Exporting Nations unilaterally raised oil prices. This action was supposedly in response to the United States' support of Israel's military buildup. For whatever the reason, OPEC's unilateral action resulted in massive price increases for oil and oil products. American consumers suffered, with

gasoline prices at service station pumps increasing three-fold over the first year. Industry fared no better.

OPEC's unilateral action also affected America's business consulting firms. By the late 1970s, General Motors, Ford, and Chrysler—all major consumers of consulting services—were impacted by the arrival of fuel-efficient Japanese and European automobiles. Low-cost imported steel and manufactured goods also contributed to the problem, as Big Steel and its vast U.S. support network stumbled. Heavy industry and the consulting firms dependent on their business both suffered.

ADL was an exception, not falling victim to the economic woes that other consulting firms endured. Over the years, ADL had developed a consulting specialty in petroleum economics. Stemming from the OPEC action and the resulting energy crisis, ADL's expertise in petroleum management provided the firm with several decades of solid growth.[9]

Nonetheless, American business practice was under fire. The Japanese aggravated an already tense situation by using its management prowess to penetrate American markets. Japanese managers not only followed practices that were successful, but they embraced a managed style that startled Americans: lifetime employment, hazy strategic alliances, worker quality circles, and their "we're all in this together" Daruma culture.

Japan's successes were worrisome enough to American businesses, but then came the Germans. German companies began complaining that the vertical organizational structure of American industries was antiquated. German businesses argued that America's system failed to take into account Europe's more complex employee situation. Rather than follow America's outdated approach, German automotive, engineering, and chemical firms began searching for their own models, in some cases reverting to their pre-war management structures. America's consulting firms – tied to American management processes – found themselves under even more pressure.

In response, American consultants began establishing fresh approaches. Boston Consulting Group typifies such initiatives.

BCG

THE BOSTON CONSULTING GROUP In 1963, Bruce Henderson founded the **Boston Consulting Group.**[10] A Harvard Business School graduate, Henderson previously headed ADL's management services unit. Under Henderson's leadership, BCG began its life as the fledging consulting arm of the Boston Safe Deposit and Trust Company. It did not take BCG long to recognize that, if it were to survive, it had to come up with its own expertise and methods.

BCG did just that. During the mid-60s, BCG developed its "experience curve" methodology, applying the method to reducing client product costs as volume increased. As expanded upon later, analysis of such "experience" provided BCG with a straightforward method useful in guiding clients in allocating their production assets and in assessing competition.

About the same time, James Abegglen, a BCG partner, opened the firm's Tokyo office. Shortly thereafter, Dr. Abegglen published his landmark "The Japanese Factory," describing Japan's unique manufacturing and employee management culture. Capitalizing on Abegglen's publications and Japanese clients, BCG established management consulting as a viable profession in Asia.

Another BCG innovation was the growth-share or, as commonly called, the 2x2 matrix. This method—discussed later in greater detail—remains a useful analytical tool in guiding strategy formation and resource allocation.

Bain & Company, another Boston consulting firm, also

BAIN & COMPANY ◄

emerged. Bain & Company was founded in 1973 when Bill Bain and a few associates left BCG.

Bain & Company built its business on client focus. Once it established itself within a client organization, Bain refused to do business with others in the client's industry. In Bain's view, avoidance of any suggestion of conflicting interest or slippage in confidentiality was paramount in building its consulting practice.[11]

More recent developments are particularly descriptive of Bain's evolution. During the 1990s and following a period of sluggish growth, Bain and its parent Bain Capital restructured ownership and incentives among its consulting partners. By the early 2000s, Bain had broadened its expertise base to include such areas as health care, information technology, media, and financial services.

About the same time, major accounting firms were developing business consulting arms. These include Arthur Andersen, Deloitte & Touche, Coopers & Lybrand, Ernest & Young, Price Waterhouse, and KPMG Peat Marwick. While these firms saw consulting as an opportunity, they came under conflict-of-interest pressure from U.S. federal regulators, causing some accounting firms to reverse course or spin off their consulting practices.

Deloitte. **Deloitte Consulting** illustrates this development. Deloitte Consulting was formed in 1995 as an arm of Deloitte Touche Tohmatsu Limited. As with other CPA firms, Deloitte entered business consulting to further support its accounting clients. Deloitte Consulting soon advanced even further, merging with major portions of Arthur Anderson's non-USA consulting business.[12]

As business consulting entered the 21st Century, consulting leadership shifted as a few consulting firms began to dominate.

- **McKinsey & Company** became one of the world's largest business consulting firms. It employs more than 17,000 consultants and professionals, with offices in 60 countries. 2013 revenues are estimated at $7.8 billion.[13]

- **The Boston Consulting Group** also became a dominant firm, employing about 10,500 globally, with 83 offices in 46 countries. Estimated 2014 revenues at $4.6 billion.[14]

- **Bain and Company** employs about 5700 professionals. It remains Boston-based. A notable associate is Mitt Romney, co-founder of Bain Capital and 2012 Republican nominee for President of the United States.[15]

- **Deloitte Consulting LLP's** 2014 consulting revenues are estimated at $11.6 billion. Revenues stem from not only business consulting engagements but also from information technology support and implementation consultants who assist clients in developing integrated solutions.[16]

- **Booz, Allen & Hamilton** segmented its consulting practice as it found its size too complex to be operated as a single entity. During 2008, BA&H separated its government and institutional business (becoming Booz Allen Hamilton) from the firm's business consulting practice (becoming Booz & Company). Change continued, as Booz & Company was in 2014 acquired by PwC. As for Booz Allen Hamilton, it further divided into two companies, with the Carlyle Group investing over $2 billion to make it happen.[17]

- **EY (or Ernst & Young)** evolved into a multinational professional services firm. London based, EY has 212,000 employees located in over 700 offices around 150 countries in the world. Noteworthy is its acquisition during 2014 of the business consulting firm Parthenon.

- **Accenture PLC** (formally part of Arthur Anderson Consulting) also developed into a multinational management consulting, technology services, and outsourcing company. Headquartered in Dublin, Ireland, Accenture reported 2013 revenues of $31 billion.[18] That portion of Accenture's revenues stemming from business consulting however, is not known.

Business consulting firms continue to evolve. An example is The Oliver Wyman Group, A New York-based subsidiary of Marsh & McLennan. The firm grew rapidly over recent years, both organically and through acquisition. Oliver Wyman had in 2014 a professional staff numbering 3700 and revenues approximating $1.7 billion.

Boutique firms are increasingly becoming significant. These niche players are building their businesses around specialized expertise or on their regional reputation. Their impact has been significant. In 2006, with annual industry revenue estimated at $125 million, the average U.S. consulting firm employed fewer than ten professionals and billed clients less than $1 million annually.[19]

Looking toward the future, business consulting firms face a mixed bag of opportunities and challenges. Firms find themselves with more demanding clients and professional staff, both better informed and with expectations higher than in earlier days.[20] Some of the more pressing challenges include:

- **Globalization.** Client needs are driving consulting firms toward globalization. Such clients insist that they receive support from consultants whose nationality and local office should mirror the client's global footprint.

  - **Networking**. In the past, senior consultants and partners within a consulting firm could pigeon-hole their research and client reports, sometimes resulting in their colleagues being unaware of the information's existence. Such narrow behavior was driven in part to protect client confidentiality. A more telling explanation was the profession's traditional partner-centric culture.

  The evolution of information technology is changing how firms communicate. The cloud, smart phones, and digital reporting have expanded the  expectations of clients and consulting staffs alike. What was once classified as client-specific proprietary information is increasingly being applied to other client engagements. Sharing the consulting firms' knowledge with its in-house professionals is becoming the rule.

- **Part-time consulting staff.** A number of factors lead to staffing client assignments with part-time professionals. One factor is the desire—even insistence—by some professionals to carve out blocks of time for their families and personal needs.

Another factor stems from economics: the need for the consulting firm to employ client-specific consulting skill without the burden of having that individual on the firm's payroll. Increasingly, consultants in possession of highly specialized knowledge are contracting themselves with several firms.

- **Teaming**. A serious test of the firm's supervisory capability lies in its ability to assemble and control individuals working in teams. Right up to the end of the twentieth century, consultants often worked alone or were captive to a particular firm's office. Going forward however, consultants work in teams. Additionally, client executives expect to be active team participants.

  Client demands are driving such teaming. Consulting engagements continue to be expensive. Moreover, clients are asking consulting firms to address geographic, political, and communication complexities not considered in earlier years. As a result of such pressures, consulting assignments can more easily go astray. Increasingly, the scoping of a client assignment is a perplexing and never-ending exercise. Likewise, time is compressed and old methodologies found wanting, all beyond the capability of a consultant working alone.

Teaming is no easy task. Team members may reside in different cities or even different countries. They might never meet face-to-face. To ensure engagement success, consulting firms are recognizing the need for their managers to be not only competent consultants, but to additionally possess supervisory and organizational skills.

Both consulting firms and their clients see teaming as a means to increase engagement success.

A Paperless World. Clients will always require reporting. Due however to the proliferation and flexibility of Power-Point and similar projectable formats, consultants are migrating away from hard-copy reports. Audiovisual presentations now rule meetings, with handouts or accompanying notes provided for later study.

As a result, paperless consulting became a game changer. No longer can a firm take a one-size-fits-all approach to its documentation. Rather, the firm's engagement manager must build into his or her work plan the client's particular reporting and information storage practices. Venues also must be pre-planned, considering which meetings would be face-to-face, which would occur during a conference call, and which would involve Skype or social media.

Disruptive Innovation describes a process by which a new product or service edges into a market only to relentlessly displacing established competitors[21]. Disruptive innovation is not new:

- The automobile disrupted the horse and buggy.
- Personal computers disrupted mainframe computers.
- Mini mills disruptive the huge integrated steel mills.
- Discounters disrupted full-service department stores.

What is new is speed of innovation's disruption, driven to a substantial extent by the accelerating miniaturization of electronic circuits and devices.[22] As the 21st century opened, the mobile phone was not only disrupting traditional land lines but began expediting internet shopping, creating a channel for social media, and driving the huge marketing and societal impact still being felt. More recently, the ongoing marriage of global positioning systems (GPS) with the internet and miniaturized electronic devices, are creating embryonic products and services so unconventional as to foster the wholly new product category called the "internet of things". Refinements and scalability of additive manufacturing will likewise be disruptive. But when? Where? By who?

Disruption of markets, products, businesses and services inevitably follow such fall-reaching innovations. But of concern to managers and business consultants alike is how best to anticipate the impact of such disruption, and even take advantage of opportunities as these come to surface.

For tomorrow's consultants, these challenges will be significant. Their significance is less in how quickly each challenge invades consulting and their clients' businesses. Rather, the larger issue is how consulting firms can best command a leadership role as things evolve.

Not changing, however, are deeply rooted consulting values. From Frederick Taylor until now, consultants have labored to devise, revise, and implement methods that best engage clients and address their issues. Consultants continue to evolve and sharpen their methodology in terms of analytical tools and all-important client communications. Regardless of a consulting firm's business strategy, its leaders know that the firm's survival and profitability hinge on the degree to which it adds value to the client.

The thoughtful consulting firm deals with this duality: drawing on  its proven methods while simultaneously seeking out and mastering challenges such as those mentioned above. Survival and growth hinges on how well each consulting firm grafts new roots onto old.

30

The Consulting Framework

Consulting firms differ. They differ in their methods, their target clients, their geography. Their differences narrow however when describing the framework they apply to solving client problems.

Practicality dictates the existence of such a framework. Clients regularly compare and select from among prospective consultants after assessing capability of each to apply the framework to the client's situation. Beyond any given engagement, consultants move smoothly from client to client. Continuing to apply this framework, professional consultants sometimes move between firms knowing that the framework is in use. If and as consultants move into business management positions, senior management expects them to bring the consulting framework to bear on their company's problems and issues. All this presupposes the existence of a framework, without which the practice of business consulting would not be as widely used and understood as it is today.

The consulting framework reflects a duality that exists between consultants and their client. Consultants are expert in assessing the present, and applying their experience to the client's problem. The client on the other hand may have no problem-solving expertise. But what the client can contribute is vision, a sense of the possible. This duality brings client and consultant provides glue holding the engagement together. It moreover bridges between the past and the future.

One component of this duality is **THE ENGAGEMENT PROCESS.** This represents the work of the consultants. In preparing for and conducting an engagement, consultants follow a three-phase process.

*1st Phase: **The Proposal.*** The process begins with the consultant developing an understanding of the prospective client's problem or issue. From that base, the consultant proceeds to structure the intended consulting engagement, and identify staffing. With this foundation, the consulting firm assembles its proposal for a consulting engagement.

*2nd Phase: **The Research.*** Once the engagement proposal is accepted, the consultants next develop their engagement plan, a rigorous focus identifying work scope, intended methods, timetable and client support. Thereafter or in parallel, the consultants select their research methodology. The actual research follows, gathering data from both client and external sources. The research phase is closed out by analysis and drawing conclusions.

*3rd Phase: **The Solution.*** The final phase of a consulting engagement focuses on providing the client with an actionable solution. The process begins by developing options and, by elimination, moves to assembling recommendations. Consultants close out their engagement by delivering a final report and, if engaged, providing support to client as it takes the recommended actions.

The engagement process is diagramed below:

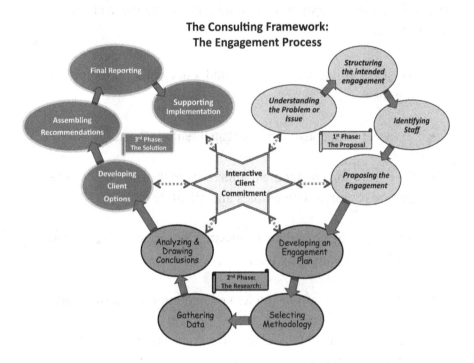

**The Consulting Framework:
The Engagement Process**

Completing the consulting framework are **CLIENT COMMIT-MENTS.** The consultant is expected to apply the most time and effort. But the client's contribution to the engagement is no less important. Consultants contribute their experience and expertise. But they cannot provide the all-important vision of what is possible within the client's organization and marketplace, and what is not. A successful consulting engagement requires that the client be committed to providing this support.

Clients contribute their commitments throughout the engagement process. Of particular importance in this regard are these client commitments:

- To select suitable consultants and, once engaged, empowering them.

- To accept the consultant's engagement proposal.

- To ensure the engagement addresses root cause, and works toward required deliverables and client deadlines.

- To accept the consultants' research and conclusions as basis for later recommendations.

- To ensure that options under consideration are actionable.

- To make decisions relative to the consultants' recommendations, and role going forward.

Taken together, the duality of interplay between the engagement process and client commitments provide the basis for the Consulting Framework, as diagrammed below.

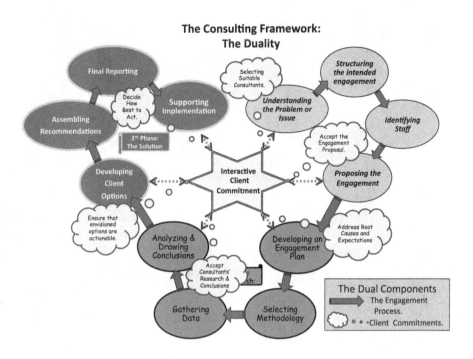

The Consulting Framework:
The Duality

Describing the consulting framework provides only a starting point. Performing within that framework is the consultant's larger challenge. The *Proposal* phase of the consultant's work is straightforward, and is described in the next chapter. The *Research* and *Solution* phases are more difficult to describe, as are the timing and appropriateness of *Client Commitments.* The challenge therefore lies in demonstrating how best to add value to the client. The following sections shed light on that challenge.

What Consultants Do:
Propose the Client Engagement

The success of a client engagement begins with its initiation. First steps generally rest with the client. The bulk of the work however rests with the consultant. He or she must generate an engagement proposal for the client's approval. In preparing the proposal, the consultant addresses a number of issues, beginning with defining the client's need.

Defining the Client's Problem or Issue

The consultant's first order of business is to understand the client's situation. While this may appear obvious, pinpointing a prospective engagement's direction and scope may be far from straightforward because:

> The problem as presented
> may not be the problem.

The client's view of its problem may, for example, be symptomatic of a larger issue. Or, the client may lay out a shopping list of issues, problems, complaints, and symptoms all stacked one upon another. Furthermore, differing viewpoints from within the client management may surface.

The consultant overcomes the challenge by digging out information that can confirm or refute that the client's thinking. If the consultant believes that his or her client is off track, the client should be so informed. The consultant should let the client know that, while he was asked to focus on issue X, the client will benefit best by attacking problem Z.

Such arm-wrestling early in the engagement can be difficult. Client management may chafe at being re-directed; they may even terminate the engagement. If the client does accept re-direction, the client's executives may wander back to their off-target definition or widen the engagement's scope. Despite the risk of early client confrontation, it is still better to deal with a wayward client early and, if need be, repeatedly. The alternative is not attractive: conducting an engagement that adds little value to the client and may tarnish the consultant's reputation.

An Imagined Engagement: Blazing Saddles Company

A fictitious example best illustrates such a situation. Meet Sam Smart. Sam is managing partner of Smart Consultants, Inc., a fictional business consulting firm. Sam has been invited to meet with the CEO (chief executive officer) of a potential client.

 *Sam Smart never cared for waiting, but waiting to meet with CEO Donna Blazer...now that was different. For the past 15 minutes, Sam had cooled his heels in the plush executive suite of Blazing Saddles Company.*

To Sam Smart, time was money. Sam was managing partner of Smart Consultants LLC. Based in Pittsburgh, Smart Consultants was a regional consulting firm experienced in addressing a diverse range of client consulting

needs. His firm had a dozen engagements under way, half of which needed his attention. He was needed elsewhere.

Still, it wasn't every day that Donna Blazer gave him a call. How many 30-year-olds were running $100 million companies? Sam knew her story. Donna had been a race horse jockey and part-time MBA student, working in her aunt's harness repair shop. Now, eight years and two rounds of venture capital financing later, she was founder, CEO and principal shareholder of Blazing Saddles Company.

Every entrepreneur in Pittsburgh knew Blazer's story. Starting from that little saddle shop, Ms. Blazer built her company into a recognized supplier to the global horse industry. Blazer's 1200 employee company made and sold not only saddles, but also bridles, boots and leather clothing to horse enthusiasts of all kinds: jockeys, rodeo cowboys, amateur foxhunt enthusiasts, horse show performers, even to the Argentinean military.

More important to Sam Smart, Blazer must be having some sort of management problem, which is why Sam willingly cooled his heals.

Sam didn't wait long. The door into the CEO's office burst open. Into the waiting room strode a blue-jeaned executive.

"Hi, I'm Donna Blazer," she said, offering her hand. "Come on in! Can I get you water, a Coke? What was your name again?"

Sam Smart reached into his pocket and withdrew his business card. He shook hands with Ms. Blazer, saying: "I'm Sam Smart, managing partner of Smart Consultants. Here's my card."

Without looking at it, Blazer stuffed Smart's business card in her jeans pocket, saying "Right, Sam, let's get to work." Blazer guided Smart into her spacious office, talking as she went."You did that marketing study for MicroSystems' new server network, right? They're a supplier of mine, you know. That's how I got your name."

Sam followed Ms. Blazer into her office. They took seats at a small conference table. "Yes", Sam replied," we consult with MicroSystems from time to time. Sorry, though, I don't think they'd appreciate my discussing any engagement."

"Yea, no problem," CEO Blazer said. "Anyway, I've got my own situation here. Can I assume we're speaking in confidence?"

"Absolutely," Sam replied.

"The last year or so haven't been much fun around here," Donna said."Our profits have dropped for the past two years. The problem is our costs; sourcing from China isn't working."

Donna Blazer went on to describe her company's venture in China. All of Blazing Saddle's leather products were produced in Shanghai. It turned out that Ms. Blazer had come up with her business idea during a China jockeying gig. It was in Shanghai that Donna saw Chinese leather goods, and recognized high quality at low cost.

"Something went wrong, seriously wrong," she continued. "Over the past year, we've cut prices to the bone, but profits keep spiraling down. Our Shanghai supplier won't give us the cost reductions they had promised. My procurement VP thinks it time to set up our own operation in China," she added. "Can you help us figure out how to do that?"

Sam listened as Donna Blazer listed her difficulties. As she told it, her problems all centered on her company's Shanghai supplier. He heard none of the usual complaints about off-quality or late shipments; nothing about the market. Things weren't adding up....

"Tell me about your competition," Sam asked. "Are they experiencing the same problem?"

"I doubt it," she replied. "We've only one competitor, that's Horses-R-Us. But their situation is different."

"Different?" asked Sam. "How so?"

"They make everything in the USA, in Chicago of all places. Goodness knows how they're able to make any money with their unionized labor costs. It's a wonder to me," she added, "Horses-R-Us just keeps growing and growing."

As Ms. Blazer laid out her competitive situation, Sam got the feeling that Blazing Saddles' problem stemmed less from their Shanghai vendor and more from being out-foxed by Horses-R-Us. According to Donna Blazer, Horses-R-Us' products were higher priced but of similar quality. Moreover, their promotional theme was frustrating: made in the USA. What really got Sam Smart's attention was when Donna opened her competitor's annual report: growing sales with good profit margins.

Blazing Saddles' CEO continued to throw out her China production ideas for another 10 minutes. Sam listened. Finally Ms. Blazer paused, then asked: "So what do you think, Can you help us plan our own China production?"

"Yes, but we may end up running in circles," Sam said.

"Would you please explain?" Donna asked.

"Running in circles," Sam repeated. "While we're focusing on your Shanghai supplier, Horses-R-Us may be further differentiating itself at your expense. It could be that, the more

energy you put into creating your own China production, the less resource you commit to battling Horses-R-Us. As I see it," Sam added, "the stronger your competitor gets, the lower the price and cost you'll need to compete. Blazing Saddles may go into a death spiral no matter what you do in China. Things might not look very pretty around here."

Ms. Blazer said nothing for a few seconds. Then she pressed her intercom button. "Get Charlie Gross and Elmer McTiernan in here please...now."

Blazing Saddle's two senior vice presidents were soon pulling up chairs around their CEO's conference table. Charlie Gross ran procurement, while Elmer McTiernan handles sales and marketing. At Elmira's request, Sam Smart repeated his skepticism about Blazing Saddles' Shanghai supplier.

"I appreciate your opinion," procurement VP Charlie Gross said, "but you don't understand the situation. We've a cost reduction agreement with our Shanghai vendor. Their costs are 16% higher than agreed when we put together our program. If we don't hold their feet to the fire, those Chinese will run all over us. Give me my own China plant, I'll show them what low cost really looks like!"

"What will you do with the improved costs?" Sam asked.

Smart's question prompted a squabble between the two vice presidents. Procurement VP Gross expected that any cost reduction should drop to the bottom line, improving profit margins. Marketing VP McTiernan went the other direction. He was equally adamant that back-to-back price reductions should follow. Bonuses were at stake for both men, Sam recognized. Neither man had any intention of backing down.

After a brief but heated give and take between her two vice presidents, Ms. Blazer said; "I've heard enough, fellows. Sam, you seem to have a handle on our situation, where should we go from here?"

"That of course is your decision," Sam replied. "But if I were in your shoes, I'd be looking for answers to not one but two questions. You're probably right that there's room for cost improvement, there usually is. It may come from your vendor, from transport, from warehousing. I'd locate areas for cost improvement, and judge how best to wring those dollars out of your product cost."

Sam looked around the table, assuring himself that the three Blazing Saddle executives were following him. "There's a second question," Sam said, "maybe the larger question. That is: how can you compete successfully against Horses-R-Us? You answer these two questions, and I believe you can craft a solution to your problem."

"Sounds good to me," ventured their marketing VP Elmer McTiernan, "but we don't have much time. In six months, we're putting on a major promotion at the international horse show in Madison Square Garden. If we're going to change direction, I need to get going."

"Change direction?" procurement VP Gross asked. "We've got to get our costs under control. Market studies are all well and good, but something's got to be done about China."

"You two will both have input to the consulting engagement if we proceed," Ms. Blazer said to her two executives. Turning to Sam Smart, she asked: "How long would it take you to finish a consulting engagement along these lines?"

"About three months. By our mid-way progress meeting, we should have a pretty good read of your situation," Sam replied. "I can probably assemble a suitable consulting team over the next week, but I need to check."

"What kind of fee are we talking?"

"Low- six figures would be my guess," Sam Smart said to CEO Blazer. "Do you want my proposal?"

"Yes," replied Donna Blazer. "I need it this week."

"I'll be back with it in a few days," replied Sam as the meeting broke up.

This example shows how consultants can guide their clients to better define their issues. Such initiative and interaction with the client increases the chance of the consulting engagement being successful. Moreover, the information gleaned from such conversation provides the basis for assembling the consultants' engagement proposal.

Before assembling their proposal, consultants will address two additional considerations. The intended engagement's activities and timing should be tentatively identified and structured. Secondly, the size, qualifications and cost of the required consulting staff should be determined.

Structuring the Intended Engagement

Proposal preparation begins with anticipating the engagement's structure. This structure is preliminary. As the engagement progresses, the engagement's nuances and complexities will call for greater specificity. Without an initial structuring however, the consultant risks preparing a proposal that fails to fit the client's situation.

The engagement's initial structure takes into account a number of variables, all based on information provided by the client. The structure should identify and sequence the engagement's major task. Further, a schedule should be developed, estimating the time required to complete each task. For complex engagements, the structure should show the inter-connection between parallel activities.

Engagement structure is typically visualized by use of an illustrative chart. Two such charts are the Gantt Chart and the PERT Chart.

A Gantt Chart[1] displays sequential tasks by use of bar charting. Gantt Charts have stood the test of time, having been developed in the early twentieth century, and brought into prominence with the advent of the PC computer during the 1980s.

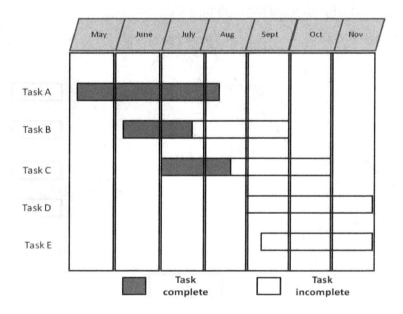

Consider the May–November engagement depicted above. Tasks are listed vertically; each task's start and finish dates are indicated horizontally. In use, the Gantt Chart is tracked and updated to visualize engagement progress.

A PERT Chart provides a more interactive structure for visualizing task progress. PERT (Program Evaluation and Review Technique) was developed by the U.S. Navy's Special Projects Office to track development of the first nuclear submarine.[2]

PERT Charts provide a tool for evaluating the impact of interrelated tasks. Of particular value is PERT's facility for identifying and engagement's "critical path", that series of tasks that requires the most time to complete. As the diagram below illustrates, a five-month engagement's critical path goes through task C.

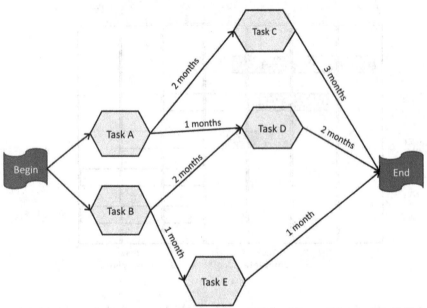

As further explanation, consider again the fictitious Blazing Saddles Company, and its CEO's request that Sam Smart's prepare a consulting proposal.

Following this meeting with the three Blazing Saddles executives, Sam Smart huddled with one of his firm's engagement managers, Jennifer Jackson. Drawing from his interview notes, Sam reviewed CEO Blazer's request that Smart Consultants study both her company's China supply structure and its competitive position. Further, Ms. Blazer needed Smart's recommendations within 12 weeks.

Together, the two consultants structured the proposed engagement. Given the need for parallel consulting paths and the tight timeline, Sam and Jennifer laid out the engagement using a PERT chart. The resulting structure is shown in Appendix A.

From the resulting PERT chart, the engagement's critical path became apparent. Four weeks were required to get into the field, and hold face-to-face interviews with those knowledgeable of this complex market and the competitive situation. Later, as the consulting team was assembling its recommendations, it would take another four weeks to meet with Blazing Saddles' nationally located marketing, sales, procurement and financial staffs, to obtain the necessary stakeholder buy-in. A 12-week engagement appeared achievable, but the schedule would be tight.

Armed with a tentative engagement structure, Sam could begin assembling his staffing plan, and, thereafter, to develop his firm's consulting proposal.

Staffing the Engagement

Consultant qualifications play a major role in staffing an engagement. The client may be a hospital administrator, for example, seeking consultants with knowledge of emergency room procedures. Or, the client CEO may require consultants with a problem-specific reputation (such as developing global supply chain strategy) to lend credibility to their recommendations.

Clients further expect their consultants to be skilled in working in and around the executive suite. During their engagement, consultants are in contact with the client organization's CEO, vice-presidents, or other executives. These senior executives face issues that cut across organizational lines. To be successful in this environment, the consultant must be comfortable working in the executive suite, and be multi-disciplined.

A team of consultants typically performs consulting engagements. Single-person staffing is not unusual, but such arrangements are generally limited to boutique or individual consulting practices. Larger and more complex engagements employ a team of consultants. Teams generally work under the direction of a partner or officer of the consulting firm. This individual oversees any number of engagements, of necessity limiting his/her involvement to project oversight and client interface.

Client engagements are typically organized along the following lines:

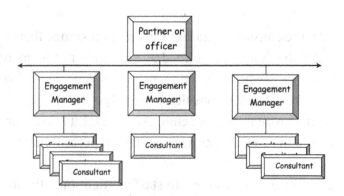

As indicated above, an engagement manager leads each team. Team makeup is usually three to five consultants in number, but may reach 50 or even 100 consultants for on large projects.[3] The engagement manager works under the partner or officer. He or she has proven consulting experience, both from a content and client-relations standpoint. One manager might handle several different clients or engagements.

Reporting to an engagement manager may be several consultants or analysts. The consultants do the work: collecting and analyzing the data, conducting interviews, and drafting reports. The more senior consultants go even further by leading client presentations and exploring possible solutions. Senior consultants may also participate in preparing proposals for future work.

Analysts sometimes assist. Analysts are entry-level staff —recent business school graduates or summer interns. They tend to limit their contributions to the analytical aspect of the engagement, with little or no client contact.

As professionals, the consulting staff is driven to maximize their billable hours. Billable hours are defined as the number of hours of a consultant's time that can be assigned to a client engagement. Too few billable hours result in the consultant or analyst becoming a drag on his or her firm's profitability. A senior Arthur D. Little partner put forth a rule that his consultants need to stay 70 percent billable.[4]

Returning to Sam Smart and his need to staff the fictitious Blazing Saddles engagement:

> Following completion of their PERT engagement outline, Sam identified members of his consulting staff who were both qualified and available to undertake the engagement. Jennifer Jackson would manage the engagement. Consultant Ben Woodbridge was available and had both supply chain and retail marketing experience. But none of his consultants had knowledge of Chinese manufacturing processes.
>
> Sam Smart did however know of a Chinese individual with such experience. George Hsu was Taiwan-based, and had a good reputation in assessing Chinese manufacturers. Mr. Hsu was a free-lancing consultant, available on a contract basis. After a few phone calls and emails, Sam contracted George Hsu to conduct their in-China tasks.
>
> Sam now was ready to prepare a staffing plan. Sam would provide oversight and be primary client liaison. Jennifer would select analytical methods, coordinating stakeholder

interviews, and prepare various reports. Ben Woodbridge would do the bulk of the field work, while contractor George Hsu would handle all in-China work.

Preparation of a staffing plan began with Sam and his engagement manager assessing each task. Task responsibility was spread across the four team members as appropriate, and the number of consulting hours estimated. From this, and applying each member's billing rate, the Blazing Saddles staffing plan evolved, as did the calculation (discussed later) of a needed $300,000 fee. Appendix B shows that staffing plan.

Armed with his engagement outline (Appendix A) and staffing plan (Appendix B), Sam was ready to develop an engagement proposal.

Developing the Engagement Proposal

Proposal assembly is no easy task. In assembling their proposal, consultants recognize three constraints: 1) the consultants' cost, 2) the consultants' time, and 3) the engagement scope. The consultants' cost refers to the consulting fee and related expenses. The consultants' time is the hours or days applied by the consultants in completing the work. The engagement scope reflects the research, field investigations, analytical work, report development, and client communication intended by the consultant.

The three constraints intertwine. The relationship between cost, time, and scope can be visualized as a triangle having legs of equal length.[5]

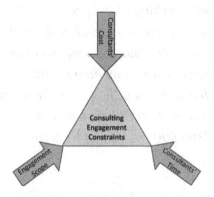

The requirement for equal leg lengths depicts the inter-dependency of the three constraints. Changing one leg of the triangle requires changing the other two.

Consultants balance these three constraints in developing and negotiating their client proposals. Does the client require a lower consulting fee? If so, the client must recognize a reduction in both engagement scope and the number of consulting hours available for doing the work. Does the client insist on lowering the engagement cost but not its scope? In that case, the consultants must either agree to provide their time at the lowered cost or walk away from the engagement. Client agreement to the consultant's proposal depends on how engagement cost, time, and scope are balanced.

The engagement fee is a major client con-
cern. Fee development begins with calculat-
ing staffing cost. Compensation required by
individual consultants is perhaps the largest
single variable. For example, an acknowl-
edged expert may command a billing rate of
$700 per hour. Analysts, on the other hand, may bill out at an hourly
rate of $100 or less. Travel and related costs are typically considered
separate from the engagement fee.

A particular engagement's fee tends to be driven by that engagement's perceived value. Clients rarely budget consulting fees. If a
budget does exist, clients hesitate to reveal the amount. Instead, clients judge the consulting fee based on the consultant's prior experiences and engagement's perceived worth.

In assembling their fee, consultants balance expected client value
against the engagement cost. By this approach, consultants determine the engagement's profit potential. Consultants may, for example, apply a 2-times (2x) markup to their costs. That markup may
drop below 2x, depending on how badly the consultants want the
engagement. Conversely, the markup may increase above 2x if the
consultants believe that their work would be of extraordinary value
to the client.

Engagement proposals will vary in format and heft. Regardless these
generally contain the following elements:

Understanding of the Client's Situation. The proposal should summarize the situation in which the client finds itself and the resultant problem or issue requiring assistance.

Intended Approach to the Engagement. Agreement must be reached on the engagement scope; how broadly or narrowly the consultants believe they must focus. Within that scope, the consultants should identify the type of research intended (data analysis, field interviews, web research, etc.), and the time frame required.

In developing their approach, consultants will draw from their engagement outline, discussed above. The outline may or may not be shared with the client, as the situation dictates. It does nonetheless provide the necessary structure at least on an initial basis.

Deliverables. The consultants will deliver actionable information to the client. The format and timing of that information depends on client needs.

Assistance Asked of the Client. Does the client possess reports, data or other information that will facilitate the engagement? Who in the client organization can or should be involved in the engagement? How frequently should meetings be held, where, and in what format? Answers to these questions will put the client on notice that its help is required over the course of the engagement.

Qualifications of Assigned Consultants. The credibility of a client proposal may hinge on the qualifications of individuals assigned to do the work. Marketing engagements for example, require marketing consultants. Or, process improvement engagements can only be conducted by consultants experienced in such processes.

The specific identity of involved consultants may or may not be revealed. Ideally, the intended consultant(s)' name and career biography should be provided. In larger consulting firms however, the logistics of staffing multiple engagements may preclude such a specific commitment prior to client commitment. Either way, the client expects that suitability qualified consultants will perform the work.

Engagement Timetable and Fee. If nothing else, the client is interested in the engagement's cost, and by when it will be completed. Earlier sections of the proposal provide the basis for both calculations. A thoughtfully assembled proposal provides the client with justification for both the consultants' fees and the engagement timetable.

Following the above guidelines, and returning to the fictional Blazing Saddles example, consultant Sam Smart calculated his firm's consulting fee to be $300,000. That calculation is shown in Appendix B. Armed with his proposal (Appendix C), Sam returned to CEO Blazer's office.

"So what's it going to cost us, Sam?" Donna Blazer asked from behind her desk. Sam Smart fished his engagement proposal from his briefcase. While only two pages in length, the document required Sam and his engagement manager

Jennifer Jackson to labor most of yesterday to get it right. CEO Blazer knows what she wants, Sam had thought. I'd better I get right to the point.

"Here is our engagement proposal, Ms. Blazer," Sam said as he handed over the two-page document. "We propose a $300,000 fee," he added, "Including expenses, the engagement would cost about $325,000."

Blazing Saddle's CEO studied Sam's proposal. "Is there any way we can lower the engagement's cost?" she asked. "I like your proposal, but money is tight around here at the moment."

Sam expected the question; had in fact prepared for it. Most first-time clients swallowed hard when hearing his fees. Repeat clients knew better, knew the value of his consulting firm's work. Sam was prepared to discuss and defend Smart Consultants' approach to the engagement. The fee could be lowered, but if Blazing Saddles insisted on a lower fee, something would have to give.

"We could work on just your competitive problem," Sam volunteered. "I suspect your China sourcing concern is real, but it may be a less fruitful area for profit improvement than dealing with Saddles-R-Us.

"How much money could that save?" she asked.

Sam checked his staffing plan (see Appendix B) and confirmed that, by eliminating George Hsu, he could cut about

$32,000 from the consulting costs, leading to a possible $64,000 fee reduction. Looking up from his staffing plan, Sam replied: "About $64,000 plus some expenses. I can sharpen that figure if you like, but your fee reduction would be in that ball park."

"I think we've got to look at both problems, both Saddles-R-Us and our Shanghai vendor costs," Ms. Blazer said. "How about we do this: let's proceed as you propose, at least until your progress meeting."

Sam looked again his Fee Calculation notes. "We will have incurred about $175,000 in fees by the progress meeting, but we'll still need to develop actionable options. My recommendation," Sam added, "is that you either accept our proposal as is, or find another way to address your concerns."

Donna Blazer drummed her fingers on her desk for a few moments before saying: "Okay, but I must reserve the right to stop the engagement following the progress meeting."

"You're the boss," Sam replied.

The client's acceptance of a consulting proposal provides the engagement's starting point. Acceptance can be as simple as a handshake. For more complex proposals where multiple clients or consulting firms may be involved, a contractual arrangement is not unusual. Regardless, consulting firms tend to proceed on a good-faith basis, in order to build and maintain trust.

*   *   *   *   *

Acceptance of the engagement proposal is only the start. As set forth in the following chapters, the consultants must now deliver well-founded and actionable recommendations. The quality of these deliverables is crucial. The consultants' recommendations may lead the client to committing itself to re-directing its business, to a major investment, or undertaking an organizational restructuring. To varying degrees, what consultants recommend can make or break the client.

The consultants also have a stake in engagement success. Obtaining the fee is important. Of equal importance is the prospect of additional client engagements and references.

Once the client accepts the consulting proposal, the work of creating and delivering value begins.

What Consultants Do:
Apply Problem-Solving Methods

Consultants focus their work by applying proven methods. Application of the right method or methods eases their task. Applying appropriate methods also simplifies client communications.

However, like the man equipped with only a hammer, every problem looks like a nail. Similarly, consultants equipped with only a few analytical methods limit their effectiveness in addressing a diversity of client problems. Selecting and ap-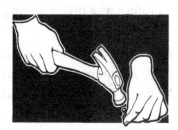plying methods is critical to providing the client with value for their money.

Other professionals face the same challenges in selecting their work methods. Consider the carpenter, responding to his customer's request to build a table. The experienced carpenter knows that his choice of tools depends on several factors. If the customer needs a backyard picnic table, the carpenter will do the job with a circular saw, hammer, and nails. However, if the customer wants an antique chair reproduced, the carpenter will forego the hammer and instead reach for his joiner, scroll saw, hand planner, and glue clamps to do his work.

Similarly, doctors, plumbers, lawyers, and artists select their tools at the outset of their engagements. Whether they work with patients, customers, clients, or patrons, these professionals know that success depends on selecting the right tools and applying appropriate methods.

Consulting methods abound. The more experienced consultants select from among these methods, usually focusing on those they understand, have previously worked for them, and best apply to the client's problem or issue. The selection of an appropriate method, therefore, is a prerequisite to providing value.

To better describe the selection of methods, a fictitious consulting engagement has been invented. In doing so, attention is given to selecting a single method that applies to a given problem or issue. In the fictitious examples below, various methods are described both from their historic perspective, and as applied to the imagined client situation.

An Imagined Engagement: Ace Construction Company

The selection and application of consulting methods can be illustrated by imagining Ace Construction Company and, with it, the fictitious consultant, Sam Smart:

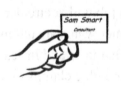 *Ace Construction Company designs and constructs bridges, highways, large buildings, and dams. Ace is a Midwestern United States company, headquartered in Pittsburgh, Pennsylvania.*

On a snowy afternoon in early January, Ace's CEO called to his office Sam Smart, managing partner of Smart Consultants. Ace needed consulting advice. The CEO told Mr. Smart

*that Ace's challenge lay in deciding how best to move dirt.
The dirt was owned by Big Bucks Casinos LLC, a gambling
consortium. Last week, Big Bucks had asked Ace to submit its
proposal to move the dirt to the proposed casino site, and
build the new Big Bucks gambling facility.*

*This was no casual pile of dirt. Rather, as Ace's CEO told
Sam Smart, Big Bucks wanted to move a whole mountaintop
of dirt, dirt consisting of gritty soil, slag rock, and dead tree
roots—the remains of a century's worth of steel mill dumping. More than three million cubic yards of dirt was involved—enough to fill ten football stadiums. Moreover, Big
Bucks needed the dirt moved from one side of the massive
Ohio River to the other. Further complicating the problem
was Big Bucks' timetable. The gambling syndicate was in a
hurry, requiring that the dirt be moved immediately so that
Big Bucks would not miss the summer vacation gambling
season.*

*As he spoke, the CEO rolled a topographical map across his
massive desk. Sam Smart leaned over the drawing. He saw
that below the mountaintop of contaminated dirt was not only
the river but also four bridges and a barge dock. The drawing showed a crayoned "X" placed a quarter-mile beyond
the river, marking the location of Big Bucks' intended Pittsburgh gambling emporium.*

The question for Sam Smart was: How should Ace move the dirt? More to the point, Ace's CEO asked, how would Smart Consultants approach the issue?

"Well," replied Sam, "that all depends....."

Applying Best Practices

Sam's probing of the CEO revealed that Ace had no experience in moving massive volumes of dirt. Mr. Smart also learned that, to the CEO's knowledge, no contractor had ever moved an entire mountaintop. Ace very much wanted this contract, but hesitated to even quote the job without having some idea of the risks associated with so massive an undertaking.

Ace's CEO asked Mr. Smart, "Can Smart Consultants determine the risks associated with such a massive earth-moving project?"

Best Practices involves locating a process, organization, or activity that is recognized as being not only effective but that, in the client's eye, provides the basis for a workable solution.

The General Electric Company (GE) developed Best Practices in 1988.[1] The method evolved as an outgrowth of GE president Jack Welsh's challenge to his company: How can GE learn from other companies, such as Ford, Hewlett Packard, and

Toshiba—companies achieving higher growth than GE? In the same manner, how could GE encourage cross-organizational collaboration among its business units? To Welsh, GE's key growth challenge was in developing and diffusing learning, no matter the source, and doing so effectively.

The Best Practices method evolved first within GE and then grew in popularity elsewhere. Its usage sometimes leads to across-the-board adoption. At other times, identification of Best Practices provides the client with a reference for deciding how to tackle a similar problem or process. The client may, for example, be less interested in "best" and more concerned with identifying other approaches to solving its problem.

Best Practices methodology can be applied broadly. For example, a nursing school applied Best Practices in researching how best to expand its on-line enrollment. A multinational equipment manufacturer used Best Practices as a guide in developing intellectual property protection in Asia.[2] Regardless of an organization's profit or non-profit orientation; management can use this method to draw on the successes of others, competitors and non-competitors alike.

From the consultant's viewpoint, the Best Practice method is particularly powerful since its application requires limited knowledge of client practices. Sales force management, supply chaining, cash management, and most other issues can be addressed using Best Practices.

Returning to the imagined Ace Construction Company:

Sam Smart and his consultants set out to locate an applicable Best Practice, to find another construction project where such a large volume of dirt had been moved. Following an extensive web search and interviews with officials from the American Society of Civil Engineers, Sam Smart learned that the Japan Port Authority of Kobe, Japan, had moved not just a hilltop, but a whole mountain across ten miles of mountainous Japanese terrain, dumping the dirt into Osaka Bay as foundation for Kobe's new airport.

Acting on this research finding, an engineering-trained consultant from Smart's staff traveled to Kobe and met with the construction firm responsible for site development. Smart was introduced to the Japanese contractor who, seeing that Ace was not a competitor, gladly shared its work plan and budgetary information. Additionally, the Japanese contractor agreed to provide Ace with engineering assistance for a fee.

Based on information gleaned from Japan, Smart assembled its proposal for guiding Ace Construction Company in moving Big Bucks' dirt. Moreover, Ace included the experienced Japanese contractor as an advisor to Ace's team. Big Bucks was impressed, and Ace's proposal was accepted.

Applying SWOT Analysis

A mountain of dirt remains a mountain of dirt. But what if management has different problem?

"...well, that all depends," replied Sam Smart. Asked why Ace Construction felt it needed help from a management consultant, Ace's CEO confided to Sam that Ace needed its earthmovers and skilled operators to remain busy during the slow winter months.

Sam Smart also learned that Ace's competitors wanted the engagement with Big Bucks for the same reason. The question was: What issues must Ace address, if the construction company was to have the best chance for winning this contract? In response, Smart decided to base his firm's consulting work on a SWOT Analysis.

SWOT Analysis[3] is a method for evaluating a client's overall business environment. SWOT's power lies in categorizing and assessing factors that, both from an internal and external perspective, are either supportive or harmful to an organization's success. The versatility of SWOT lies in its simplicity.

Albert Humphrey, while working at the Stanford Research Institute, created SWOT. These four letters stand for the following:

- **S**trengths, representing those internal factors which give the business unit a competitive advantage;

- **W**eaknesses, or the internal characteristics placing the business unit at a disadvantage;

- **O**pportunities and other external situations enhancing the business unit's competitiveness; and

- **T**hreats, representing those problems that might arise from the outside world.

A thoughtful SWOT Analysis provides the client with a moment of truth. Is the client heading for trouble? Do conditions allow the intended strategy to succeed? By constructing a SWOT analysis, consultants can guide their clients in assessing the strategic and tactical reasonableness of intended actions. SWOT is typically visualized according to the following table:

	Helpful to the client:	Harmful to the client:
Internal to the Company:	Strengths	Weaknesses
External to the Company:	Opportunities	Threats

Consultants apply the SWOT method when the client has a clear goal but is uncertain as to its pathway. For example, the client may need a plan to head off a crisis, but lacks an understanding of the surrounding landscape. In this case, SWOT Analysis provides a method for identifying where preventative action is required. The client may also apply SWOT to profile competitors prior to market entry and anticipate competitive reaction.

The worth of this method rests in its out-of-the-box potential. SWOT Analysis takes the client beyond what it traditionally understands, drawing attention to forces internal and external, historical and prospective.

Returning to the imagined Ace Construction Company:

> *Sam Smart described SWOT to the CEO, explaining how application of the analytical tool can guide Ace's decision. By focusing on SWOT as Smart's primary consulting method, the Smart Consultant won the consulting engagement.*

> *As his first step, Sam developed information necessary to perform his SWOT analysis. That input came from interviews with Ace executives, Big Bucks' staff members, government officials, local trade union executives, and individuals familiar with competitive construction activity. Armed with this information and engaging help from Ace executives, the Smart Consultants built a SWOT model along these simplified lines:*

Ace's Strengths:	Ace's Weaknesses:
Ace was the area's most experienced dirt-moving contractor.	Ace possessed no experience in transporting dirt across a large body of water.
Ace's Opportunities:	**Threats to Ace:**
No other construction company had sufficient equipment on hand to begin the work on short notice.	Competitor Warner Contractors had built numerous casinos for Big Bucks and was developing its own proposal.

Drawing from this SWOT assessment, Smart and its client concluded that they should approach Turner Contractors as a joint venture partner. Ace agreed and reached out to Turner Contractors. Within days, the two companies jointly issued a proposal to Big Bucks and won the contract.

Applying the Hypothesis-Driven Model

Or, what if management sees a different issue?

"...well, that all depends," replied Sam. Through his questioning, Sam Smart learned that Ace's CEO had no idea as to how to satisfy Big Bucks. Big Bucks was already late in opening its Pittsburgh casino, so was insisting that the dirt-moving job be completed in four weeks so that the Pittsburgh casino could open by Easter. The CEO wondered how the tight deadline could be met. Ace Construction Company had enough earthmovers to complete the work in ten weeks, but

70

four weeks? The CEO and his managers were at a loss as to how to proceed.

Sam Smart decided to involve several of his engagement managers into thinking through Ace's dilemma. A few days later, Ace's CEO repeated the problem to Sam Smart's staff and fielded their questions. After conferring, the consultants believed that Ace should focus on working quickly, not on minimizing cost. If Ace could lay its hands on a massive number of barges and trucks, and work their operators around the clock at barging the dirt across the river, Ace had a shot at meeting Big Bucks' four-week completion window.

Smart called for another client meeting, during which time Smart proposed that Ace Construction Company focuses on determining how fast it could move the dirt by barge.

However, Ace's CEO still had concerns. How could Smart Consulting determine that barging could do the job—and within the four-week timeframe?

By applying a Hypothesis-Driven Model, Sam explained.

The Hypothesis-Driven Model[4] is associated with McKinsey & Company, management consultants. As applied, a solution (the hypothesis) is laid out at the outset, and then tested and re-tested by following a process similar to that diagrammed below:

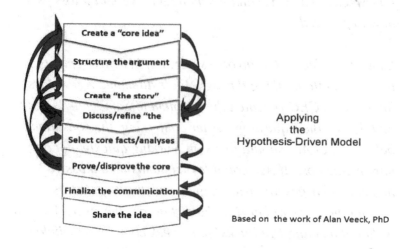

Create a "core idea"

Structure the argument

Create "the story"

Discuss/refine "the

Select core facts/analyses

Prove/disprove the core

Finalize the communication

Share the idea

Applying
the
Hypothesis-Driven Model

Based on the work of Alan Veeck, PhD

According to the diagram, Hypothesis Modeling devises pathways to a solution. Once the problem is understood, the consulting team begins breaking down the problem into component elements and judging which elements drive the problem. The model further assists consultants in identifying their data needs. It is through this process that Hypothesis Modeling leads to a solution.

McKinsey, a major practitioner of Hypothesis Modeling, applies the method to large client organizations facing complex strategic challenges. In practice, McKinsey attacks such problems through a three-prong, problem-solving process. That process includes not only use of Hypothesis Modeling, but developing a strong factual basis and working inside a rigid consulting structure.[5]

Returning to the Ace Construction Company example:

Following Sam's explanation, Ace's CEO bought into using Hypothesis Modeling. He gave Sam Smart the go-ahead to undertake a feasibility study. The Smart consultants then adopted the core idea of minimizing time, since Big Bucks was more concerned with an Easter opening than with construction costs. The Smart consultants defended this hypothesis, on the basis that a slower timetable worked in favor of less expensive competition and risked the freezing of both the Ohio River and the mountaintop.

As the consultants hypothesized, Ace would work 24/7 over the course of four weeks. Ace would also lease every available barge and earth-moving truck, and authorize double and triple overtime when necessary. By keeping to this schedule, Big Bucks could begin casino construction by late February.

To prove or disprove the hypothesis, the consultants undertook a wide range of investigations. They studied historic weather patterns to insure a 24/7 availability of waterways, roads, and bridges. After learning that too few barges were available, the Smart Consultants revised their core idea to include the leasing of out-of-state trucks.

Smart orchestrated a pre-bid meeting that included Ace, Big Bucks, and Smart's consulting staff to test the hypothesis. Big

Bucks liked the hypothesis, leading Ace to use the information gleaned from Smart's Hypothesis-Driven Model to prepare its dirt-moving proposal. Big Bucks awarding the earth-moving contract to Ace who began work the following week.

Applying Porter's Five-Force Competitive Model
Or, what if management's concerns revolved around competitors?

"...well, that all depends," replied Sam Smart. On further  *probing, Smart learned that Ace did most of its work outside the Pittsburgh region. Consequently, Ace's CEO was unfamiliar with local competitors. However, Ace Construction Company did want to develop more Pittsburgh business. Big Bucks provided that opportunity.*

As best Ace could judge, three local construction companies and several out-of-state contractors would bid on the Big Bucks' dirt-moving job. Additionally, smaller contractors could band together to bid on this attractive job. How Big Bucks viewed the competitive landscape was anyone's guess. Ace Construction Company needed help in assessing its competitors.

Listening to Ace's CEO revealed to Sam Smart that Ace's management was unable to answer key questions about their competition. Should Ace's bid be stand-alone, or were local partners called for? Were local political connections a fac-

tor? Did any competitor have the inside track, thus making Ace's efforts a waste of time? What should Ace do?

Smart decided that, if Ace were to win this engagement, his consulting firm would apply the Porter Five-Force Competitive Model.

Harvard Business School's Michael Porter developed this method.[6] Porter's premise is that profitability is neither random nor industry-specific. Rather, an industry's profitability can be predicted by assessing five competitive behaviors. The diagram below illustrates Porter's model:

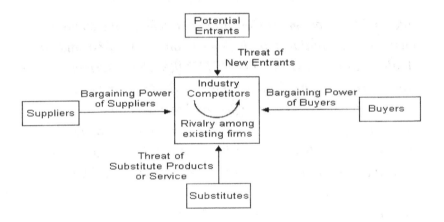

In practice, consultants apply Porter's Five-Forces Model as one method to help evaluate the attractiveness of a client's business strategy. According to Porter, attractiveness relates to a given market's profit potential. An attractive market is one with limited competitive activity. When few competitive forces come into play, profit potential is substantial. Too much competition, on the other hand, leads to a competitive free-for-all, driving down the profitability for all competing firms.

The thoughtful consultant recognizes that the Porter Five-Force Model usually provides only a starting point. Because Porter's method is qualitative, it does not address other specifics such as organization structure, supply chain, or the program's profit potential. Additional methods—Value Chain Analysis or Net Present Value Analysis, for example—may be put to work to flesh out and quantify the consultant's assessment.

Returning the Ace Construction Company example:

> *Ace's CEO asked Smart Consultants to take on the engagement. As their initial step, the Smart consultants first studied Ace's local INDUSTRY COMPETITORS who, it turned out, were in various phases of exiting the construction business. The problem was that the region had few BUYERS and these consisted of governmental construction projects, each of which was heavily influenced by local politics. Smart Consultants did not give importance to SUPPLIERS of building materials, contracted labor, and leased vehicles. However, Smart Consultants did view POTENTIAL ENTRANTS as a threat, mainly from Delaware Contractors, Inc. located across the state. As far as SUBSTITUTES were concerned, a Canadian manufacturer was promoting an elevated people-moving system that could move gamblers back and forth across the Ohio River, leaving the pile of dirt where it was.*

Working with the Porter Five-Force Competitive Model, Smart advised Ace to move aggressively on the earth-moving opportunity. Ace thereupon submitted a minimally priced bid and pulled out all stops to gain endorsement from local politicians. Ace got the order.

Applying the 2x2 Matrix

Or, maybe management is stymied by an even different problem:

"...well, that all depends," Sam Smart replied before asking, "What else can you tell me? What are the issues here?"

Ace's CEO leaned across his desk and said, "The question focuses on how we should move the dirt. I prefer trucks, but the folks at Big Bucks think that conveyor belts are the way to go. My engineering staff likes neither trucks nor conveyors; they favor the economics of barging. If we don't all get on the same page and act soon, we'll lose this job."

"How are you going to handle this?"

"That, Sam, is where you'll earn your money," Ace's CEO said. "I'm giving you the engagement, hoping that you'll figure it out."

Sam Smart set out to do just that. As his first step in the engagement, Sam needed to narrow Ace's dirt-moving options and do so in a way both credible and descriptive. Sam decided to apply a 2x2 Matrix.

The Boston Consulting Group (BCG) developed this unique 2x2 Matrix as a response to those clients concerned about the relative performance of their several business units.[7] BCG's four-quadrant matrix compares two of a business unit's characteristics, for example industry attractiveness with its competitive position. The two axes of the resulting matrix gauged market growth (indicating industry attractiveness) and market share (indicating competitive strength).

As interpreted by BCG consultants, the resulting four quadrants gauge profitability and cash flow, and imply strategic direction. As depicted below, BCG labeled the four quadrants as Dog, Cash Cow, Star, and ???:

The Boston Consulting Group (BCG) Growth-Share Matrix

- **Dog business units** are a drag on the client's business. Dogs are characterized by low or unstable earnings, sucking up.

management time and energy. Cash flow may even be negative. The implied strategy is to divest.

- *Cash Cow business units* pay the client's bills. They have
  high and stable earnings, and a strong cash flow. The implied
  strategy is to use the cash to fund other initiatives.

- *Star business units* are where the client's future lies. Stars
  have high and stable earnings, and are growing. The implied
  strategy is to invest.

- *??? business units* are a dilemma to the client, these units
  have low or unstable earnings but are growing nonetheless.
  The implied strategy is to deal with these business units on a
  case-by-case basis.

As with any method, the 2x2 Matrix has its advantages and limitations. Key advantages include ease of preparation, capability for
simplifying complex situations, and clarity of presentation. The 2x2
Matrix provides such a platform.

The 2x2 Matrix method can be stretched. A three-dimensional matrix can for example be developed: the 2x2x2 Matrix, providing
eight quadrants capable of assessing three characteristics across eight
quadrants. Additionally, consultants can place images on the matrix,
using size (volume, dollars, etc.) or position (more or less) as further
description.

Consider for instance the procurement needs of a multi-national chemical company. That company's question is: Which of its material suppliers need monitoring, particularly given the company's limited staff resources?

In response, management sets up a 2x2 Matrix that compares supplier stability with the impact of that material on the company's business. As an enhancement, each material's usage is indicated, showing both dollar purchases and changes over time. The resultant matrix provides a straightforward depiction of the situation. It shows, for example, that attention should be given to the purchase of butane acid:

The 2x2 Matrix
applied to procurement planning

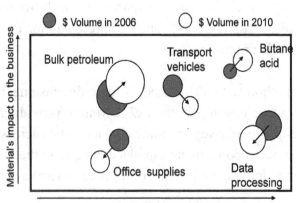

The 2x2 Matrix also has limitations. Its very simplicity downplays complexities, such as business linkages and synergies among business units.

Returning to Ace and the fictitious consultant Sam Smart:

> *Applying the 2x2 Matrix, Smart Consultants set out to assess Ace's dirt transport options. Three transportation issues were identified: cost, the time required to move the dirt, and potential disruption to river traffic. Regarding costs, the Smart consultants learned the following:*
>
> *Cost of trucking the dirt: $85,000.*
> *Cost of barging the dirt: $27,500.*
> *Cost of conveying the dirt: $45,000.*
>
> *The time required also varied. Trucking the dirt could be accomplished in one month, by far the fastest option. Barging took the most time, requiring seven months to move the mountain of dirt from one side of the Ohio River to the other. Conveying the dirt could be completed in five months.*
>
> *The use of conveyor belts was viewed as the most disruptive dirt-moving option, given the time and cost required to erect the necessary mid-river support pillars. Barging involved a range of administrative difficulties due to policing by the U.S. Coast Guard. Although trucking the dirt would not be disruptive, this option was clearly the most expensive. Using this information, the Smart consultants built a 2x2 Matrix:*

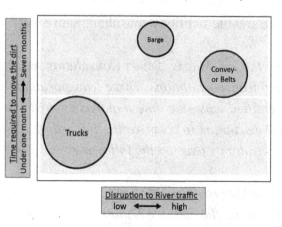

Ace Construction Company:
Assessment of dirt-moving options
(Each option's cost reflected by size of circle)

When presented with the above 2x2 Matrix, Ace's CEO became excited: he now had a tool for bringing the parties together.

During the next few days, the staffs of Ace Construction Company and Big Bucks LLC held a pre-bid meeting. Using the 2x2 Matrix, Ace presented the dirt-moving options. A lively discussion ensued.

Following a brief break, Big Bucks announced that, all things considered, trucking was the way to go; river disruption posed too many political implications. Thereupon, Ace set out to assemble its dirt-moving proposal.

Applying the Six-Sigma DMAIC Model

Or, the consultant hears yet a different client concern:

"...well, that all depends," replied Sam Smart. Sam had learned that Ace had considerable experience in moving masses of dirt. Although transporting the material was not a concern, cost control was. Ace had lost money on recent earth-moving projects. Unless Ace's CEO could show that this contract would result in a profit, Ace's CEO doubted if his Board of Directors would support the Big Bucks' construction project.

Ace's CEO asked, "Can Smart Consultants show us how to contain our costs?"

"I believe so," Sam replied. "Have you ever heard of the Six-Sigma DMAIC model?"

Two analytical frameworks make up this method. Edward Deming developed the DMAIC framework, for use by the Japanese automobile industry.

DMAIC[8] provides a means for streamlining workflow by pinpointing ways to improve the various manufacturing processes involved. The five initials stand for the five steps of **D**efine-**M**easure-**A**nalyze-**I**mprove-**C**ontrol, and are described as follows:

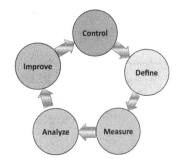

- **D**efine the goals of the project. Such goals may include increasing market share, raising output, and improving customer satisfaction. Agreement on goals provides the basis for defining success before the work begins.

- **M**easure the current level of performance. Measurement provides a baseline against which to gauge progress as process improvements are implemented.

- **A**nalyze the discrepancies between goals and actual performance. A variety of statistical tools can be applied to better understand cause-and-effect relationships and to better ascertain the costs of making improvements. During this step, management assesses the value of reaching Six-Sigma quality levels, or of pursuing a less costly but lower performing route.

- **I**mprove existing systems through project management methods and via dialogue with the organization. Progress monitoring may require that statistical measurements be put into place.

- **C**ontrol implementation of change and change's impact on the organization. Success requires more than implementing new methods and better processes. To be successful, changes also need to be managed to head off any negative or counterproductive impact. Instituting new controls further ensure that changes survive.

In practice, DMAIC is usually coupled with the Six-Sigma framework. Six-Sigma was developed by Motorola. The term "Six-Sigma" refers to a statistical confidence that the level of process defects is only three in a million. Like DMAIC, Six-Sigma provides a set of practices. Six-Sigma aims to reduce process variations and, by doing so, minimizing waste or defects. The General Electric Company established the worth of Six-Sigma when, in 1998, it announced cost savings of $350 million as a result of applying Six-Sigma methods to its processes.[9]

The combined Six-Sigma DMAIC method applies primarily to larger clients—those companies having more than 500 employees. Because smaller organizations have fewer needs, they tend to rely less upon the Six-Sigma DMAIC methods. Smaller units further lack the trained staff (referred to as Black Belts) needed to apply the method and monitor project success.[10]

Returning to Ace:

> After receiving Ace's go-ahead to apply the Six-Sigma
> DMAIC method, Smart's consultants first defined what costs
> were acceptable to Ace. Smart then measured the mountain
> of dirt, adjacent roads, bridges, docks, and barging facilities.
> Ace also collected labor rates and vehicle operating costs.
> Furthermore, Smart analyzed recent earth-moving projects,
> looking for discrepancies between Ace's original budget and
> actual costs.

With this information, Smart developed an improvement pro-
gram focusing on the control of operator overtime. In his fi-
nal report, Smart's recommendations not only proposed
these improvements, but also established controls that pro-
vided Ace management with daily reports comparing actual
versus forecast overtime expenses.

Ace implemented the improvements and controls generated
by applying the Six-Sigma DMAIC methodology. As a result,
Ace completed the Big Bucks' dirt-moving project on time
and well under budget.

Applying Pareto's 80:20 Principle

Or, management expresses a totally different problem:

"...well, that all depends," replied Sam
Smart. Further questioning by Mr. Smart
revealed the Ace's CEO was unsure that
he could rely on his skilled equipment
operators. Never before had Ace asked its operators to han-
dle earth-moving equipment during the frigid winter months.
Until now, Ace had avoided winter work, allowing its opera-
tors some downtime while collecting unemployment
compensation.

As a result, Ace's CEO needed answers. What must Ace do to
motivate its 120 unionized operators to move the Big Bucks
dirt? Does Ace risk being unable to fulfill its earth-moving
contract and having to pay penalties? How can we gain an

understanding of operator sentiments when so many of them were wintering in the deep South?

Sam Smart knew how to approach the problem: by applying the century-old Pareto 80:20 Principle.

Early in the twentieth century, Italian economist Vilfredo Pareto studied Italy's wealth distribution.[11] Pareto found that only 20 percent of the population owned 80 percent of the Italian land. He further observed that, to his surprise, 20 percent of  his garden peapods yielded 80 percent of the harvested peas. Pareto continued his research and, over and over again, uncovered the same phenomena.

These and other observations led to an analytical tool that stands the test of time: the Pareto 80:20 Principle which states that 20 percent of an effort provides 80 percent of the result.

In practice, Pareto's ratios may be 75:30, 85:20, or some other ratio marginally similar to 80:20. But the larger the database, the closer the relationship approaches 80:20. For example:[12]

- Eighty percent of computer run-time comes from twenty percent of the lines of code;

- A carpet company finds that twenty percent of its leased carpeting accounts for eighty percent to ninety percent of carpet wear;

- Twenty percent of a company's sales force produces about eighty percent of the company sales; and

- Roughly eighty percent of a retailer's customer complaints stem from twenty percent of the retailer's products.

Consultants make use of the Pareto 80:20 Principle when available data are buried in a large and diverse population. Without such a simplifying method, the consultant risks information overload and paralysis, resulting in the consultant's inability to draw meaningful conclusions or make timely recommendations. Application of the Pareto 80:20 Principle facilitates faster solutions with greater client buy-in.

Back to Sam Smart and his imagined Ace Construction Company client:

Drawing on the Pareto method, Sam Smart and his consultants began by studying Ace's equipment operator records. Smart learned that 24 of Ace's 120 equipment operators had performed 85 percent of the previous year's work. On showing this analysis to Ace managers, they agreed that these 24 were representative of their total number of operators. Accordingly, Smart sought out and interviewed Ace's 24 top equipment operators. In short order, the Smart consultants concluded that the unionized opera-

tors would return to work during February, but requiring a
20 percent wage premium for doing so. Accepting this wage
assumption, Ace felt comfortable in developing its dirt-moving
proposal.

Applying Decision Tree Modeling

Or, the client's situation is entirely different than first realized:

"...well, that all depends," replied Sam
Smart. On further questioning, Ace's
CEO revealed to Sam that Ace's man-
agement was divided as to the best way
to transport dirt across the Ohio River.
A few executives endorsed barging as the least expensive
method. Others, however, were concerned about the river
freezing, since the work would be done during February.
Should the river freeze, they argued, Ace would have to bear
its contractual barging cost and pay for trucking.

Ace's CEO then asked Sam Smart: "How can I bring both
groups into agreement?"

"Your situation lends itself to Decision Tree Modeling," Sam
replied.

Decision Tree Modeling comes into play when, for each possible
outcome, probabilities for success can be developed.[13] This method
is particularly useful in assessing a broad range of options and opportunities, and turning the related data into actionable knowledge.

The simplicity of the Decision Tree Model drives its flexibility and usefulness. A Decision Tree provides a visual structure for inspecting possible outcomes. Overlaid on this structure are each outcome's expected value or cost, and the outcome's probability for success. Given the model's tree-like structure, consultants frequently display their Decision Tree on marker boards or through PowerPoint to facilitate communications. Additionally, computer simulation offers an endless array of permutations and analytical possibilities.

Returning to Sam Smart and Ace Construction Company:

> *As the first step in constructing Ace's Decision Tree Model, the Smart consultants determined that trucking the dirt would cost $85,000. The cost of barging would be $27,500. The consultants further learned that, historically, the Ohio River was frozen solid across 12 percent of past Februaries. Armed with this information, the consultants built the Decision Tree below:*

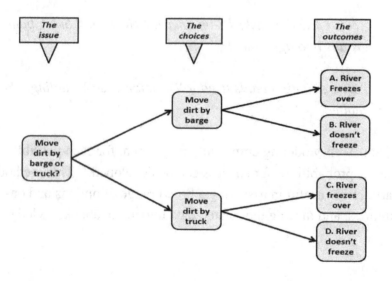

The Smart consultants next calculated the Expected Cost (EC) for Ace Construction Company's two choices.

- *Choice One: Move Dirt by Barge. The Expected Cost (EC) for this choice is the addition of the ECs associated with outcomes A and B.*

  ○ *Outcome A's EC is 0.12 x ($27,500 + $85,000) = $13,500.*
  ○ *Outcome B's EC is 0.88 x $$27,500 = $24,200.*
  ○ *Total EC for outcomes A or B = $37,700.*

- *Choice Two: Move Dirt by Truck. The condition of the river does not affect the Expected Cost, hence the Total Expected Cost for Outcomes C or D = $85,000.*

Smart Consultants advised Ace that, by barging, Ace should expect to be ahead by $85,000 less $37,700, or $47,300. Based on this, Ace Construction proposed barges for the river crossing.

A variation of decision tree modeling is **decision mapping.** Mapping is based on diagrams similar to those used with decision trees. Mapping focuses however on identifying options and weighing their relevancy. Qualitative assessments may be applied to these options, but the numbers are typically not decisive. Rather, decision mapping's value rests in its visuals, providing the client with a compelling diagram that pulls together the major variables affecting the required business decision.

Given an appropriate client situation, decision mapping provides consultants with methodology both valuable and efficient. Consider for example a manufacturing client concerned about an unrelenting loss of customers. Variables affecting that client problem might be mapped along these lines:

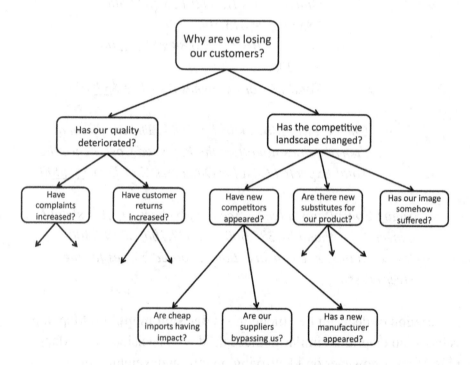

In the above example, the consultants focus their research on identifying the variables, and assembling a reflective decision map. In doing so, they probably introduce other methodologies such as Porter's five-force competitive model to better frame the client's competitive situation. Once assembled, the decision map provides the consultant with a credible tool for guiding client management toward an appropriate and timely decision.

An interesting adaptation of decision mapping is the **Pyramid Principle.** The Pyramid Principle was developed by Barbara Minto, during her consulting work at McKinsey & Company.[14]

Applying the McKinsey 7-S Model
Or, the client's issue is more organizational in nature:

"...well, that all depends," replied Sam Smart. As Ace's CEO laid out his problem, Smart became concerned about the availability of suitably qualified professionals to conduct the engagement. The more he listened, the more Smart realized that his consulting firm could not help Ace.

"We really want to work with Ace," Smart said to Ace's CEO, "but my consultants are currently committed to other clients. I would be glad to recommend another consultant, if that would be helpful."

"I appreciate your candor," replied Ace's CEO, "and thanks for taking the time to see us." He paused before continuing. "Can you take a few more minutes, and tell me about your consulting practice? We may have other needs."

Sam Smart explained that his firm had built its reputation by helping businesses deal with organizational upheaval. "Let's take acquisitions as an example," Sam said. "Most corporate acquisitions fail.[15] Strategic alliances and joint venture partnerships don't do much better. It is our belief that a major source of the problem stems from clients failing to understand how their organizations actually work or don't work. We make our money by helping clients avoid organizational failure."

"How do you do that?" asked Ace's CEO.

"By paying attention to the elements driving an organization's success," Smart said. "We like to apply the McKinsey 7-S Model. 7-S helps us gauge our client's readiness to deal with change."

Sam Smart was referring to the McKinsey 7-S Model. Tom Peters and Bob Waterman,[16] consultants with McKinsey and Company, developed this method during the 1970s. Their model assumes that organizations consist of more than just formal structures. Rather, Peters and Waterman believe that organizations consist of seven elements, as the following diagram identifies:

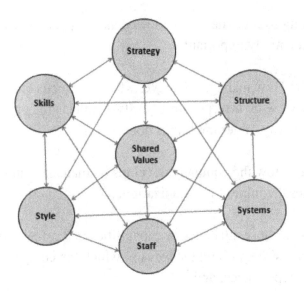

Three of the seven elements are "hard" and, therefore, easy to identify:

- **Structure:** How people and their work are organized, reflected in the organization's hierarchy and mechanisms for implementation and specialization;

- **Strategy:** Those commitments that a company is based upon and intends to follow, regardless of how the environment changes; and

- **Systems:** The various processes and information flows that tie together the organization.

The remaining four elements are viewed as "soft" elements less observable but equally important:

- **Style:** How managers behave, what they focus on, and how they view their responsibility. Style reflects the organization's way of getting things done;

- **Staff:** How the company develops its managers and integrates them into the organization;

- **Skills:** Those attributes or capabilities that reflect the company's strengths and the ways in which the company builds its competencies; and

- **Shared Values:** Those visions and standards that shape how a company conducts its business and controls its destiny. These values may not be readily apparent to outsiders.

In their research, Peters and Waterman further uncovered that the more successful companies pay attention to all seven S's. Failure to pay attention to the four "soft" S's—Style, Staff, Skills, and Shared Values—was particularly disruptive to the success of acquisitions, mergers, or alliances.

The 7-S Model has demonstrated success in optimizing the performance of a company's organization. Consultants will apply the method to anticipate the likely effects that planned changes will have upon their client's organization. The 7-S Model also provides structure for assessing and aligning business unit departments and processes following the combining of two organizations. Whether it is applied to re-organization, merger, or acquisition, the 7-S Model provides a tool for determining how best to change a client's complex organization.

Returning to consultant Sam Smart and his client Ace:

> *"Maybe you can help us in a different way," Ace's CEO said to Sam Smart. "We recently acquired an equipment leasing company, figuring that it could help us streamline our earthmover scheduling and, as a bonus, find customers wanting to rent our equipment during slow times."*
>
> *"How has the acquisition panned out?" asked Sam.*
>
> *"A disaster," replied the CEO. "Those guys are a bunch of prima donnas. They don't like getting their cufflinks dirty, and don't understand preventative maintenance. It seems that every time a major issue comes up, all we do is argue. Now that I think about it, that bunch of yo-yos could torpedo my Big Bucks project. With guys like that around, that contract could blow up in my face!"*
>
> *The conversation between Sam Smart and Ace's CEO moved forward, ending in Ace giving Smart a consulting contract to identify organizational issues existing between Ace and its newly acquired leasing company, and to recommend improvements. During the following weeks, and in an effort to*

understand Ace's 7-S Model, Smart consultants interviewed executives, suppliers, and customers.

Two issues became apparent. Ace and its acquired leasing company operated entirely different reporting systems, with Ace intent on tight scheduling and its leasing subsidiary focusing on contract profitability. Additionally, the two business units' operating styles differed. Ace valued rough-and-ready field engineering, leading to macho management and a 'blue-jean-style' back office; these styles were at odds with the leasing subsidiary's 'wing-tip shoe' mentality.

"Take a few days off with both management teams," Sam advised. "Play golf together, and bring in an experienced facilitator to begin guiding the two organizations toward a common 7-S organization model. It won't happen overnight, but at least you'll have begun to recognize each organization's drivers."

Ace's CEO and his senior staff accepted Smart's recommendations. Maybe Ace could make the acquired leasing company successful after all.

Applying an Experience Curve

Or, the client's concern is more operational:

"...well, that all depends," replied Sam Smart. "Why not just quote your best price, and take your chances?"

"I wish it were that easy," replied the Ace CEO. "But if we quote based on what little experience we have in moving dirt, our price is bound to be uncompetitive. We'd lose the contract bid for sure."

"So why are we having this conversation?" asked Smart.

"Because my guys tell me that, after a few weeks on the job, they can reduce costs big-time. My question to you is this: how do we cost out this project, based on experience we don't yet have?"

Sam considered the question. He then began describing to Ace's CEO a methodology called an Experience Curve.

The Boston Consulting Group (BCG) developed this methodology during the 1960s.[17] Working with a computer chip manufacturer, BCG saw its client's production costs fall about 25 percent every time it doubled in volume. After doing additional research, BCG confirmed that a cause-and-effect relationship did in fact exist between cumulative output and unit cost.

BCG developed the Experience Curve, a compelling and uncomplicated method for guiding clients in production planning. The outline below shows the Experience Curve:

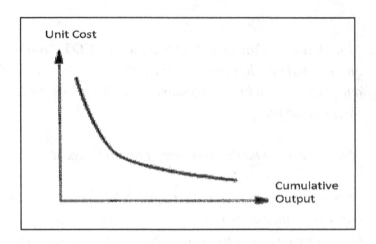

Consultants apply Experience Curves over a wide-range of volume-related activities. The method has obvious uses in manufacturing planning. An Experience Curve can impact other areas as well. The method can, for example, provide a basis for developing market leadership by timing the introduction of expensive advertising and enlarged sales coverage.

Returning to Ace and consultant Sam Smart:

> *Ace's CEO liked the idea of using an Experience Curve as the basis for its cost projections. The next day, Smart consultants teamed up with Ace engineers. The team developed a dirt movement schedule—Ace's cumulative output—that covered the entire assignment. Working backward from this forecast, Smart and his team built up an Experience Curve and, in doing so, were able to estimate the cost of moving dirt along each step of project progress. These data provided the*

basis for developing and proposing Ace's cost estimate to Big Bucks for moving the dirt.

Ace won the contract. More importantly, Ace not only lowered its dirt-moving costs as it gained experience, but Ace did so along the lines of its anticipated Experience Curve. Ace turned a significant profit on what had been a risky undertaking.

Applying Scenario Planning

Or, the client lacks a clear picture of where it is heading:

"...well, that all depends," replied Sam Smart. "Moving dirt seems like a fairly straight-forward undertaking, particularly given Ace's construction experience. Tell me more about your concern."

Ace's CEO leaned back in his big swivel chair and, clasping both hands behind his head, stared at the ceiling. "We really want this job. If we're successful, two more casinos may follow."

"Big Bucks sounds like a good customer to me," Smart said.

"Maybe, maybe not," replied the CEO. "They're letting things move too fast. They have yet to decide where to build their first casino. Heck, Big Bucks purchased options on half

*the vacant land in Pittsburgh! I can move dirt all right, but
not if Big Bucks won't tell me where to put it!"*

*Smart understood the anxiety of Ace's CEO. How could Ace
submit its dirt-moving plan when Big Bucks provided no destination? As Smart knew, such ambiguity arose both inside
and outside the business world. For example, who could have
foreseen the 2011 Arab Spring, and where social media had
taken the Arab world? What might the two Koreas look like
under new leadership?*

*Smart recognized that both geo-political situations led to
the same problem facing Ace: anticipating change, change
so disruptive that past events provide little basis for
planning.*

Smart decided to apply Scenario Planning,[18] a system first developed
by the Rand Corporation. Following the 1950s' Korean conflict, the
U.S. Department of Defense asked Rand to develop a means for describing the future in ways both persuasive and easy to understand.
Scenario Planning evolved, providing a qualitative technique for assessing and promoting likely outcomes.

Scenario Planning lends itself to a broad range of issues. Early in the
1970s, the oil company Royal Dutch Shell applied the method to
counter the global threat of ocean-going oil tanker overcapacity.[19]
Clients facing tactical decisions have also benefited from Scenario
Planning by using the method to determine the impact of game-
changing technology on a given marketplace.

In practice, Scenario Planning begins by identifying those goals and realities driving the organization's future. To do so, Scenario Planning considers the organization's history, competitor practices, market forces, and governmental activity. Brainstorming also plays a central role during deliberations. The method's value lies neither in generating a set of numbers nor in detailing the future. Rather, Scenario Planning's value is as a consensus builder, and uncovering predictive milestones.

Like no other consulting method, Scenario Planning provides a tool for transforming confusion into commitment, apathy into excitement. Which scenario is the most robust? Which provides the strongest opportunity for contingency planning? Which scenario motivates executives into seeking that pot of gold?

Returning to the Ace Construction Company example:

The Smart consultants went to work, applying Scenario Planning to Ace's problem. As a first step, Smart studied the sites of other casinos owned by Big Bucks, particularly those built recently. Sam Smart's consultants then interviewed Big Bucks' management and architects, as well as Pittsburgh city fathers, to gain insight into site selection criteria and preferences.

Following this work, and in collaboration with Ace's management, the Smart team of consultants fleshed out three casino site scenarios:

- **Scenario One:** The dirt is graded into a flat-top pyramid atop the largest available acreage, with the casino built atop;

- **Scenario Two:** The dirt fills the huge ravine dividing the city's center, with the casino located mid-ravine; or

- **Scenario Three:** The dirt builds an island in the center of the Ohio River, creating a destination casino.

Following Sam Smart's guidance, Ace's CEO provided Big Bucks with three separate proposals, one for each scenario. For each, Ace Construction Company assembled a table-top model and identified the associated economic, social, and political issues. For each scenario, Ace also estimated the cost of moving dirt, preparing the site, and constructing the casino.

A heated discussion followed, with Big Bucks' executives arguing for their favorite scenario. After an hour of discussion, Scenario Two began gaining traction. By day's end, the Big Bucks' team threw its weight behind locating its Pitts-

*burgh casino in center-city. More importantly, Big Bucks
awarded Ace the dirt-moving contract.*

Applying Other Methods

As the following list illustrates, additional problem-solving methods
abound:

- *Net Present Value*[20] calculations compare the cash flow generated by different programs operating across differing time-
  frames. NPV is particularly useful in marketing or business
  planning engagements, where a common basis is needed for
  evaluating future but different time frames.

- *Fishbone or Ishikawa Diagrams*[21] are used to visualize and
  isolate cause-and-effect variations in complex situations.
  Applications include designing products, isolating manufacturing defects, and addressing environmental variations.

- *Logic Trees*[22] can graphically break down a complex problem. The method's value is in guiding the client from
  problem definition though analysis, progressing to the in-
  spection of alternatives, and then moving the user across
  the method's tree-like structure. In doing so, Logic Trees
  provide a structured and well-reasoned tool for addressing
  complexity.

- *Value Chain Analysis*[23] inspects the series of activities upon
  which a business's products or services depend. The resulting
  analysis provides the user with a basis for determining the

collective value of these activities. Value Chain Analysis is particularly valuable when assessing a client's capability to support a new market initiative.

- *Game Theory*[24] analyzes the interaction between individuals dependent upon each other. In business, Game Theory is used for zero-sum gaming, where one organization hopes to gain what its competitor loses.

- *Voice of the Customer*[25] (VOC) is a market research method. As applied, VOC captures customer expectations, preferences, and dislikes. This qualitative method is based on structured interviews VOC generates—information that adds credibility to a consultant's market assessment work, thereby helping clients deal with market ambiguities

- *Hierarchy of Needs Theory*[26] was developed by Abraham Maslow. In one of the oldest consulting methods still in use, Maslow in 1945 theorized that a person matures or deteriorates by moving between five steps of need satisfaction. The basic need is physical and, once satisfied, progresses onward through safety, belonging, esteem, and finally to self actualization. Management consultants apply Maslow's Theory in strategic or organizational engagements, when clients need to understand employee response to changing business situations.

- *A Spider Chart* gauges the value of options when multiple variables come into play, and does so graphically. As shown in the adjacent example, each of the several variables is gauged by extending axes from a center 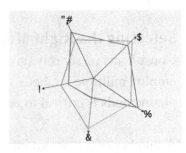 point, all starting from a center point. Spider charting has particular value as a display technique when comparing complex opportunities such as selecting between multiple acquisition candidates.

- *Gap Analysis* is a method for identifying the steps required to advance a dysfunctional program to a desired future objective. The method's value rests in its three-step simplicity: (1) identify those critical factors (such as success benchmarks, resource availability, etc.) that define the current situation, (2) list the totality of factors required to meet the future objective, and (3) identify the "gaps" existing between (1) and (2). Consultants apply this method when the client's endgame is clear, but the pathway to success is unclear.

Selecting the Right Methods

Consultants rarely rely on a single method. More frequently, they employ multiple methods. The decision to apply one, two, or multiple methods is critical to engagement success.

A number of factors go into method selection. Selection typically begins with the consultant considering his or her familiarity with any given method. However, the nature and depth of the client's concern is of greater importance. In deciding between methods, two questions are pertinent:

- **Question One:** What is the intended client action? Perhaps the client has tactical concerns, facing problems such as how best to organize, how to get where it needs to go, and how to benchmark success. Or, the client must make strategic choices, such as the nature of the business it should enter, the assets it needs, and sources of new capital.

- **Question Two:** How difficult is it to apply a particular method to the client's situation? The consultant's expertise, the time available to complete the engagement and availability of relevant information drive this consideration.

Armed with answers to these two questions, the consultant can begin selecting a method or methods that support the client's requirement. The 2x2 matrix below facilitates that selection.

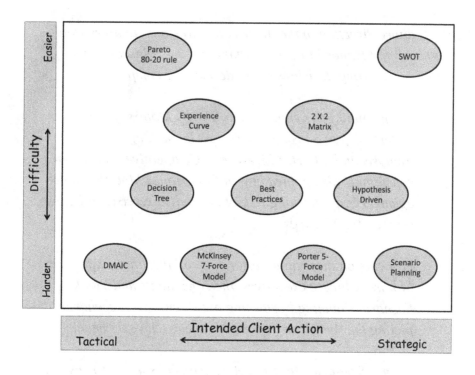

The following fictitious example exemplifies the value of applying multiple methods:

> *China's Honey Motors asked its consultants to prepare Honey Motors to compete in the American auto market, and to do so by envisioning how that market might appear in the year 2030. Such a long view was important to Honey, since a diverse range of management decisions waited that positioning: vehicle design and performance characteristics, sources of financing, overseas staffing, dealership arrangements, supplier alliances, and multi-national organizational considerations to name a few. For Honey Motors, these decisions were not casual. Rather, how Honey Motors defined the*

future direction of the American auto manufacturers would commit Honey Motors for years to come. Moreover, too many wrong decisions could destroy the company.

Upon winning the engagement, Honey Motors' consultants undertook a two-prong assessment by building a SWOT Analysis and a Porter Five-Force Competitive Model. The consultants also gained buy-in from Honey Motors's management by performing risk-opportunity exercises utilizing several 2x2 Matrices.

Drawing on these analyses and in collaboration with Honey Motors' Chinese executives, the consultants undertook Scenario Planning by fleshing out three market scenarios depicting the American automobile scene ten years hence:

- **Scenario One:** *The American consumer returns to a made-in-USA preference;*

- **Scenario Two:** *American automakers cease making cars and become importers; or*

- **Scenario Three:** *American automakers succeed in reducing their costs and emerging as significant auto exporters.*

These three scenarios provided the basis for the consultants to guide Honey Motors's top management discussions. In the end, Honey Motors decided to commit to the third scenario, believing that American automakers will again become significant automobile exporters. Honey Motors thereupon began assembling a program to take itself to 2030. Of equal importance, it identified benchmarks for tracking the American industry's progress (or lack of) toward the selected scenario.

As shown in the example above, effective consultants draw on a range of analytical methods. Which methods should they ultimately select?

Well, that all depends.

What Consultants Do: Deliver Value

Clients pay consultants to deliver value. This value is built on more than just the final report. As described below, value delivery begins early and is continues across the entire engagement.

Delivering Value: By Engaging Client Stakeholders

Client leadership stems from more than one or two executives. Their success in solving a problem or issue stems from that handful of executives' ability to move others toward a common client goal.

Consultants cannot view client management as a shapeless mass. Rather, consultants perceive these individuals as "stakeholders." Stakeholders are individuals within the client organization whose jobs are affected by how their organization deals with the situation under study. Three types of stakeholders are considered:

> **Supportive stakeholders** are individuals who would benefit from successful completion of the consulting engagement.

> **Conflicted stakeholders** are individuals whose jobs or personal interests might be endangered by the engagement's results.

> **Gatekeepers** are individuals who control access to information vital to the engagement progress. They may be supportive or conflicted.

Early in the engagement, effective consultants identify who among client management falls into which stakeholder category, and develop the means to deal with each. Regardless of the stakeholder's attitude, the consultant's task is to move all stakeholders toward accepting the consultant's eventual recommendation.

Influencing stakeholders is a continuous process. It requires the consultant to include stakeholders in every facet of the process. Although full agreement among client stakeholders may never be attained, the consultant nonetheless works toward stakeholder consensus. As the engagement progresses, stakeholders may for example change their view of the situation. While a source of frustration, this shifting is constructive. Changing stakeholder opinions reflect the reality that the client's business is in motion.

Client meetings provide a useful vehicle for guiding stakeholder thinking. Meetings provide the consultant with an opportunity to explain chosen methods and how these methods were selected. As data are uncovered, consultants can apprise the stakeholders of progress, and provide stakeholders with an opportunity to respond. Though such communication, the consultant's final recommendations should surprise no one.

Delivering Value: By Developing an Engagement Plan

A thoughtfully prepared engagement plan guides the consultant toward a successful completion. The consultants begin developing their plan following their initial client meeting. Key components of a typical engagement work plan are examined below.

Understanding of the current situation:
Does the consultant appreciate the state of
the client's business affairs, and the variables that drive the client to bring in a consultant? The client needs to know that its
consultants begin with that understanding.
Assembly of a broad historical review is
unnecessary. Rather, the consultant should
prepare a concise summary, providing the

consultant's description of the relevant business climate in which
the client operates and competes. The value here is in establishing
the consultant's credibility, as someone who understands the
stakeholders' situation.

Description of the client's problem or issue: A successful outcome
requires a precise description of the problem or issue. A client "problem" for example might be that Product A's profit margins are declining. An "issue" might be that the client lacks credible acquisition
criteria. However described, the consultant's initial meetings with
the client must provide the basis for a clear description.

Obtaining clarity is rarely a straightforward exercise. Consider the
product profitability problem mentioned above. The consultant may
find that, rather than getting to the point, the client prefers to dwell
on company history ("we're losing money"), or voice the problem's
symptoms ("The company hasn't paid a dividend in two years"). Or,
the several executives briefing the consultant may portray the problem totally different.

Experienced consultants expect such distractions. These can be re-solved through dialog with the client. Their techniques for managing the client conversation include re-phrasing the problem, questioning client assumptions, and probing for details. Through such dialog with the client, the consultant separates the noise of history, the temptation of attacking symptoms, and unraveling any tangled think-ing. Here, the value added by the consultant is in helping the client focus on the root problem. An example consulting engagement plan is provided as a template in Appendix D, and as an example in Appendix E.

Understanding the Client's Desires and Expectations: Managing client expectations are critical to engagement success. The client wants a solution to its problem or issue. Solutions are rarely "yes" or "no" answers. Rather, the solution rests in a blend of three components.

1st: *The specific engagement objective.* The objective should identify the kind of solution the client is seeking. For example, in resolving the problem of declining product profit margins, the client may be-lieve that its solution will be found by:

- Identifying those components in the product's value chain that are represent the greatest factors in margin decline, and thereby recommending corrective action,

    or

- Identifying those customer markets showing the greatest de-cline in profit margin, and recommending corrective action, or

- Doing both.

As with agreeing on the problem, describing with the engagement's objective results from discussions with the client.

2nd: *A measurement or validation of success*. Given the client's objective, the next component is capturing the client's view of a successful solution and how success will be measured.

Documenting that view differs between quantitative and qualitative client objectives. Describing success for a more quantitative objective (such increasing revenues or reducing costs) is usually straightforward: dollars saved or margin improvements for example.

Validating success for a more qualitative objective may better be explained than measured. Take for example a client asking its consultant to assemble a pathway for upgrading the client's product development effectiveness. In this case, the client's hoped-for success might be validated when the first new product demonstrates its game-changing impact on the marketplace. Another validation could be when the recommended pathway is endorsed by the affected client stakeholders.

3rd: *The expected timetable for success*. This third component deals with the client's expectation regarding success timing. Let's say for example that the client's wants to reduce its manufacturing costs by

40%. But by when does the client expect these results…next month? Next year? In five years? Agreement at the outset of the expected timetable for success provides client and consultant alike with a necessary reference for assessing the opportunity, cost and risk associated with implementing any change.

Gaining a client's agreement on its expectations can be challenging. Reason is that different clients bring different experiences and bias to their consulting engagements. It is not unusual for the client to expect the consulting consultant to research all related topics, interview any and all individuals that might contribute, and develop the optimal solution. While laudable, such an expectation may prove undoable. Consultants work under budgetary and calendar constraints. Given those limitations, consultants can add immeasurable value by leading their clients to seek not the "best" solution but a solution that is workable.

Another challenge could be differing opinions among client stakeholders. Their differences may be casual, with the consultant needing to bring individuals together on a single issue. On the other hand, the consultant may be faced with stakeholders with wildly differ views on not only the consulting engagement's objective, but also the nature of and timetable for success.

Finally, the client may never have given much thought to the nature of the solution it is seeking. Client stakeholders may understand and agree on their problem. Their expectations relative to the engagement outcome may however be vague or even non-existent. The experienced consultants will not shy away from this dilemma.

Rather, they will take the initiative to guide the client's thinking, and facilitate client stakeholders in reaching consensus on these critical components of the engagement plan.

How the Consultant Intends to Proceed, which includes:

Scope of Work, which represents the intended research, field work and analysis. From where do the consultants intend to get their information? Is field work required and, if so, why and where? What input or involvement is required from client staff? The answers to such questions provide the consultants with their basis for scoping out their engagement.

Intended methods and analytical framework. Here, early choices by the consultant are important. The consultant's research and field work will feed into the selected analytical model or method. Different methods however require different kinds of data or information. Consider for example how the consultant's research will differ, should he or she decide between applying a Porter Five-Force Competitive Model or a decision tree or a SWOT analysis.

Engagement Schedule and Tasks: Consultants learn early in their careers that, unless they organize themselves well, time expires before their work is completed. To avoid this, consultants will assemble a time-sensitive schedule.

The engagement schedule draws from a number of factors. The consultant begins by reviewing the intended engagement structure set forth during pre-engagement proposal preparation, as was discussed early. Thereafter, and after developing a thorough description of the engagement and client expectations, the consultant is in a position to develop a schedule which addresses these questions:

- What specific tasks should be undertaken?
- When should these be completed?
- What obstacles or challenges are expected in doing this work?
- What dates and benchmarks are key to completing a successful engagement?

Answers to these and similar questions provide the basis for an engagement schedule and a descriptive listing of major and related tasks.

Information required from the Client: The consultant needs to identify and obtain copies of relevant data and reports held by the client. Should field interviews be intended, the work plan should request the client to suggest sources and make introductions. Additionally, obtaining internal clearances and signing non-disclosure agreements may take time and, therefore, should be completed at the engagement's outset.

Key Contact Information: The consultant should gather and distribute to all engagement participants, their email addresses, telephone numbers and other contact information.

Engagement Budget: This final aspect of the engagement plan deals with reimbursing consultants for their out-of-pocket costs. This includes foreseen air travel, lodging, meal, rental car and similar travel costs. Other costs may be fees paid to contract consultants, the purchase of published reports, and printing costs. Such reimbursement is typically provided separate from the engagement fee.

The decision to share with the client all or a portion of the engagement plan rests with the consultant. The consultant judges which plan assumptions and commitments require confirmation with the client. Some clients may wish involvement in all aspects of engagement planning. Others may want little to do with engagement planning, asking only to see results. Whatever the consultants decide, they must satisfy themselves that their engagement plan is appropriate to the client's needs, and adds value.

Delivering Value: By Gathering Useful Information

Without information, the consultant offers little more than speculation. Good data breathes life into the consultant's methodology. Consultants derive useful information from a variety of sources, including the following:

- **Information from the client.** The client can be counted upon to possess useful information. Annual reports, market plans, customer reports, personnel assessments, and other internal documents provide the consultant with a starting point. Pursuit of prior studies and reports in the client's possession is important. Such information provides the consultant with insight into the engagement.

The client however may not be supportive. It may have already studied the problem, but may have lost the report or forgotten it even exists. Or, believing that "objectivity" is best served by concealment, the client may withhold information. Experienced consultants understand and anticipate such situations.

- **Information from published reports.** Various governmental agencies issue reports. These documents may cover a wide range of topics, including financial information filed by the client or by the client's suppliers, customers, and competitors. Federal, state, and regional agencies issue far-ranging studies on all sorts of topics. The U.S. State Department, the U.S. Central Intelligence Agency, and the United Nations all offer fertile ground for research. Non-profit organizations, including trade associations and lobby groups such as the American Chamber of Commerce, provide an additional source of information. Initial research into such data sources can begin with a web search. Thereafter, direct contact may be required.

- **Information from client-specific surveys.** Consultants can initiate quantitative surveys when surveying large populations. Consumer market engagements lend themselves to such research. Applying such surveys however demands that the consultant to possess considerable expertise in areas such as population selection, questionnaire design and administration, and statistical assessment and interpretation. To convince the client to act on such surveys, the consultant must have both intuitive and statistical confidence in the results.

Delivering Value: By Getting the Most from the Method

Once selected, an engagement's analytical method(s) is as valuable as the consultant makes it. The various problem-solving methods discussed earlier all have proven value. A method's value to a particular engagement however depends on the consultant's skill in adapting method to situation.

An example illustrates. The fictitious Watanabe Medical Center wants to acquire additional hospitals. It wishes to acquire up to three hospitals that service Massachusetts. To assist with their decision, two consultants are hired: #1 and #2. Each consultant is told to work separately. Each  has the same assignment however: evaluate three acquisition candidates identified by Watanabe, and recommend how best to proceed. The three candidate hospitals are Narragansett General, Fall River Community, and Cape Ann Regional.

Both consultants selected a 2x2 matrix as their assessment and presentation method. To gather required information, Consultant #1 began by interviewing Watanabe's administrative staff, and researching Watanabe's prior acquisitions. He determined that two criteria were utilized in making past selections:

1. Hospital size as measured by number of hospital beds, and

2. Hospital profitability.

Based on these two criteria and using data obtained from the consultant's research, the following 2x2 matrix was assembled and presented to Watanabe senior staff:

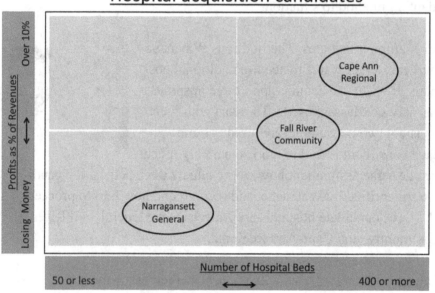

Assessment by Consultant #1:
Watanabe Medical Center
Hospital acquisition candidates

Based on this assessment, Consultant #1 recommended the acquisition of the larger and more profitable Cape Ann Regional Hospital.

Consultant #2 dug deeper. Like Consultant #1, she meets with Watanabe senior staff and studies Watanabe's past acquisitions. Additionally, Consultant Two interviews Watanabe's chief financial officer, as well as its various department chiefs. She confirmed that Watanabe wishes to acquire hospitals which are both sizable and profitable. Additionally however, Consultant #2 finds Watanabe less interested in acquiring a hospital's profitability than in its ability to sustain itself with its own cash flow. Additionally, Watanabe's nationally recognized oncology staff is actually driving the acquisition initiative. Their ambition: to create a world class oncology surgical team.

Consultant #2 thereupon develops three variables as key to the Watanabe acquisition initiative:

1. Hospital size as measured by number of hospital beds,

2. Cash flow, and

3. Relative size of the candidate hospital's oncology surgical staff.

She then produces this 2x2 matrix:

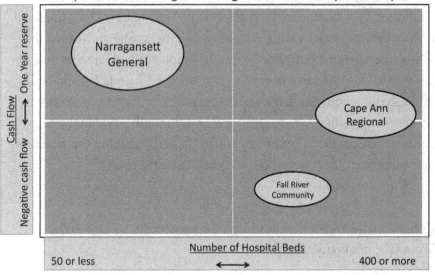

Assessment by Consultant #2:
Watanabe Medical Center
Hospital Acquisition Candidates
(Relative Size of surgical oncologist staff reflected by circle size)

Based on this assessment, Consultant #2 advises Watanabe Medical Center that no candidate meets all criteria. Narragansett General and Cape Ann Regional do however merit consideration. While smaller, Narragansett had a recognized oncology surgical staff and generates significant cash. Cape Ann on the other hand is only marginally cash-sufficient. Cape Ann is however a large hospital albeit with a small oncology surgical practice. As for Fall River Community, that hospital falls short and therefore should be rejected.

Comparing the work of the two consultants, Watanabe senior staff is impressed with Consultant #2. Consultant #2 worked with not two but three acquisition criteria. In addition, Consultant #2 displayed a greater understanding of Watanabe's needs. Consultant #2 consequently is asked to continue assessing Narragansett and Cape Ann hospitals. In Watanabe's view, Consultant #2 added the greater value and is expected to add even more.

Delivering Value: By Conducting Face-to-face Interviews

Information takes the consultant only so far. Client reports provide a starting point. Published data lacks specificity. It was also developed in support of a mission different from the client's. Surveys provide insight, but into what?

Consultants often undertake field interviews to complement data and, more importantly, to validate and provide specificity to the consultants' recommendations. Consultants seek interviews with individuals knowledgeable about a significant aspect of the client's problems or issues. Such individuals may belong to government or trade associations. They may also be executives with client customers, vendors, or partners. Individuals working within the client organization are also important sources, particularly in explaining or expanding information provided during the engagement kickoff.

During marketing engagements, consultants may need to interview client competitors. Competitor interviews simultaneously represent the most fruitful source of information and the most difficult interviews to arrange. When contacted, competitors raise questions: Why should they talk with you? Why should they give information to an organization that wants their company's business?

The experienced consultant, anticipating these questions, can respond in two ways: 1) My client is prepared to share what we have learned with you, and 2) You now have the opportunity to influence my client to stay away from your market. Competitor interviews are best conducted late in the interview process, when the consultant has a better understanding of the client and its issues.

Interviews are held face-to-face or by telephone. Face-to-face interviews provide more candid responses, particularly if the consultant can build rapport. However, face-to-face interviews are more difficult to arrange and, once scheduled, require the time and cost of the consultant getting to the interviewee's location.

Telephone interviews are easier to arrange, but may lack context. Telephoning can be impersonal, discouraging the exploration of new ideas or better data sources. As a result, consultants seek face-to-face interviews whenever possible.

Unlike telephone interviews, face-to-face interviews require the consultant to combine aggressive outreach with a carefully crafted interview plan. The consultant's plan should:

- Assemble a product or services description;
- Develop an interview questionnaire;
- Identify individual to be interviewed;
- Organize and conduct interviews;
- Summarize what was learned; and
- Draw conclusions.

How the consultant sets up and carries face-to-face interviews requires a combination of careful planning and forceful execution. For the more qualitative engagements such as business-to-business marketing, successful interviewing is crucial to engagement success.

An Imagined Engagement: XYZ Fluid Control Company

The mechanics of face-to-face interviewing is best described by an example, returning to fictitious consultant Sam Smart. This time, Mr. Smart is working with a different client—the XYZ Fluid Control Company.

XYZ Fluid Control Company manufactures industrial filtering devices used in the metal working industry. Headquartered in Pittsburgh, Pennsylvania, XYZ prides itself on being the industry's technical leader in developing filters capable of handling changing production requirements.

Recently, XYZ's engineering department completed design of an innovative approach to oil filtering. XYZ calls the resulting product its "Widget." The Widget was developed in response to requests from customer metal fabricators for a filter capable of removing microscopic carcinogens from metal cutting oils. Although it took XYZ several years to do create the Widget, the result was a patented filter system new to industry, capable of removing practically all contaminants. By installing Widget, XYZ believes that its customers will be able to do away with environmentally hazardous settling ponds and costly contaminated oil disposal.

Before moving forward with the XYZ Widget, CEO Fred Glitch insists that his business planning staff first justify the $10 million cost to set up Widget manufacturing. For its part, XYZ's planning staff believes that the investment would payback in two years.

However, the XYZ planners had doubts. They felt too ill-informed to develop a reliable market entry timetable or reliable sales outlook. Lacking insight into evolving customer requirements and competitive activity, XYZ's planning staff could go only so far. For these reasons, XYZ decided to engage consultant Sam Smart. His assignment was to confirm and complete XYZ's net present value (NPV) analysis of Widget's profit potential. The initial work performed by the XYZ planners is shown below:

	Widget Net Present Value (NPV) Analysis: Based on internal XYZ information							
	Expected Widget Market			XYZ profit margin potential in this Market				
	Units (000)	Price Per unit	Market size ($mil)	XYZ Market Share	XYZ Sales ($mil)	Profit Margin %	Profit Margin ($mil)	Profit Margin NPV @ 9%
Year 1	5	$500	$2.5	100%	$2.5	40%	$1	$1
Year 2	50	$500	$25	100%	$25	40%	$10	$9
Year 3	100	$500	$50	75%	$37.5	40%	$15	$12.2
Year 4	???	???	???	???	???	???	???	???
Year 5	???	???	???	???	???	???	???	???
							Forecast 5-Year NPV of Profit Margin Stream	???

Sam's first step was to huddle with XYZ's business planning staff to assemble a Product Description.

Product Description:

The XYZ Widget

General description: The Widget is a patented filtration system, for use by metal fabricators in removing carcinogens and other microscopic contaminants from lubricating oils. The Widget is intended to replace traditional oil filter systems, which are unable to filter sub-micron materials. By replacing existing filters with the Widget, customers can eliminate the need for environmentally hazardous settling ponds and costly disposal.

Weight: 24 pounds

Materials: stainless steel and proprietary inorganic filters

Installation requirement: standard two-inch piping to handle in and outflow; installation by the customer

Power: 220 Volts AC

Reduction in flow volume during filtration: less than 0.1%

Results of filtration: sub-micron: 99.7%; larger particles: 99.9%

Maintenance: none during warranty period

Warranty: Five years

Price: $500 per unit

Commercial availability: In 6 to 9 months

Consultant Smart then met with XYZ's sales management to develop an Interview Questionnaire. According to Mr. Smart, information provided by answers to these questions should lead to actionable recommendations.

Interview Questionnaire
Drilling Oil Filtration Market

Interviewee name, title, organization_____

Contact information: telephone, email_____

I.

The Market for gang drill tooling:
– What is current industry filter practice? Need, available technology, trends?
– Who are the major customers? Their location? Their annual purchases?
– What companies supply oil filter systems? Their share of market? Their price?

II.

Distribution Channels:
– What is role of suppliers, distributors, and/or representatives in the supply chain?
– What distribution mark-ups are typical?
– Are local inventories required? Consigned stock? How important are spare parts?
– Who performs field service: Factory? Independent service providers? In-house by customers?
– What fees are charged?

IV. Potential Competitors to XYZ's Widget:
– Which filter system makers are most likely to offer a product similar to the Widget?
– What development is each working on? What is state of development? Any trials underway?
– How do these competitors compare with XYZ? Strengths? Weaknesses?

V. Interviewee's evaluation of the Widget:
– What are the Widget's advantages? Disadvantages? Areas for modification?
– What is your opinion of XYZ's intended pricing?
– What is the potential value to customers of the Widget? Why?
– What technical or service support would customers expect?
– Which metal working customers are most likely to purchase Widgets? At what volume?

VI. Additional observations provided by Interviewee:
– Who else should be interviewed? What insight can they offer?
– Does the interviewee know of existing studies or reports that would be interest?

As final preparation before commencing interviews, Smart worked with XYZ management to identify individuals capable of answering Sam's questions. Sam knew from experience that informed interviewee would rarely resist an opportunity to discuss a subject—any subject—about which they were well informed. On that basis, Smart and XYZ assembled a list of interview candidates.

List of Intended Interviews			
XYZ Personnel	Houston, Texas Sales office	Jon Hoffman, Sales Manager	Referred by Fred Glitch
	St. Louis, Missouri Sales office	Hugh Howe, Sales Manager	Referred by Fred Glitch
	Home office: Engineering Dept.	Jim Crane, VP Design	Referred by Fred Glitch
	Home office: Cost Estimating	Will Willis, Cost Director	Referred by Fred Glitch
Potential Customers	Alpha Products, Houston, Texas	Mary Jones, VP Materials	Referred by Fred Glitch
	Beta Systems, Dallas, Texas	Jack Smith, Product Mgr.	Referred by Fred Glitch
	Gamma Solutions, St. Louis, MO	Stu Spenser, VP Production	Referred by Fred Glitch
Trade Association	National Filtration Association, Washington, DC.	Gary Smith, President	Referred by Fred Glitch
Competitors to XYZ	ABC Filter Corp, Cleveland, Ohio	Anne Smith, VP Sales	No contact, a cold call.
	DEF Fluid Control, Cleveland, Ohio	Mike Frost, CEO	Referred by Fred Glitch

Armed with the XYZ Widget Product Description, the Interview Questionnaire, and the list of Intended interviews, Consultant Sam Smart went to work. Smart figured that he needed about two weeks to complete his interviews, assuming that interviewees would not only meet with him, but also adjust their calendars to fit Smart's travel schedule.

His first telephone call was to Mary Jones, vice-president of materials at XYZ's major customer: Alpha Products of Houston, Texas. Sam dialed Ms. Jones number.

"Mary Jones' office, Julie speaking," the voice answered. "May I help you?"

"This is Sam Smart calling," Smart said. "I'm a management consultant helping XYZ's president Fred Glitch evaluate an improved cutting oil filtration system, Fred asked that I get input from Ms. Jones."

"Her schedule is pretty tight," replied Julie. "How much time would you need?

Sam Smart had a ready answer. "I would appreciate a half-hour of her time. I plan to be in Houston two weeks from now. How does her schedule look on the 31st?"

"I'll check," the young lady said. A minute passed before she returned to the phone. "Ms. Jones wonders if you are available on the 30th in the late afternoon."

After checking his schedule, Smart replied, "I'll be there at 4:00 p.m., and I'll confirm by email."

In a similar fashion, Sam Smart set up the rest of his interviews. His schedule began in Houston with the Alpha Systems interview on the 30th, followed by meetings in Dallas and back to Houston the following day. On the 1st he scheduled his St. Louis interviews; he ended the week in Cleveland. The following week, Smart would hold interviews with XYZ management.

Sam Smart entered Alpha Product's Houston headquarters on the 30th at 3:45 p.m., giving himself time in the lobby to study the Widget questionnaire. Promptly at 4:00 p.m., Sam was escorted to the office of materials vice- president Mary Jones. He returned the questionnaire to his briefcase before entering her office.

"Thank you for your time," Smart began. "Fred Glitch believes your insight into XYZ's new filtering system will benefit both of you."

"XYZ has been a good supplier to us," Mary Jones said. "However, I've not much time, and I'm not sure I can be helpful. What do you need to know?"

Smart opened his briefcase, withdrawing his notebook and the Widget product description. He handed the description to Ms. Jones. During the next five minutes, the two of them discussed features of the Widget.

"What do you think?" Smart asked.

"What I think," she replied, "is that Jacob Schulz should hear about this." Jones pressed her intercom and said, "Please ask Jacob to come here. I've something he'll like to hear about."

Four p.m. went to 4:45 p.m. as environmental engineer Jacob Schulz joined the meeting. Two more engineers and a cost manager entered the conversation. During that time, Sam Smart was able to obtain answers to most of his questions. As the clock approached 5:00 p.m., Jones turned to Smart.

"When can we have one of these...what do you call them...Widgets to test?"

"I don't know," replied Smart. "I'll check with XYZ..."

"Vice-President Jones cut in: "I'll check with XYZ myself. We need this device yesterday; if Fred Glitch wants to keep our business, he'll ship us a Widget when we say so."

"What's your hurry?" Sam Smart asked.

"The Federal EPA just slapped us with a shutdown injunction, closing one of our carcinogen disposal sites. We've got to figure out a solution yesterday," she said before adding, "Our interview is over. Sorry."

Sam Smart closed his notebook and stood up. "Can I ask you a few quick questions on the way to your next meeting?"

Glancing at her watch, Ms. Jones said, "Walk down the hall with me; I've a meeting with our CEO. We can talk as we walk."

During the next few minutes, Sam and Ms. Jones walked down several halls and climbed two sets of stairs. Ms. Jones invited Smart to sit with her in her CEO's waiting room. Before Mary Jones had to rush away, Sam Smart gained several additional insights. In particular, he learned that the EPA's shutdown order was national, not just in Texas. He also learned that none of XYZ's filter-producing competitors had a clue as to how to help Alpha Systems or anybody else. Lastly, and probably the most importantly, Ms. Jones told Smart that Alpha was willing to pay $700, or maybe more, for a product that performed as described by the Widget product description.

Sam Smart was soon back in his car and writing up his notes. Next he would head for Dallas and his hotel.

Tomorrow's interview with Beta Systems should be interesting, Smart thought.

Two weeks later, Sam Smart had completed his field interviews. As luck would have it, Smart had succeeded in interviewing his entire list and gaining solid answers to all his questions. Smart had met face-to-face with them all, except for the DEF Fluid Controls whose CEO took Smart's telephone call from the her Arizona vacation home.

As his final step in the interview process, Smart summarized his research. A number of findings appeared particularly relevant, which he presented to his client:

The market needed XYZ's Widget and needed it now;

1. *Widgets appeared salable at $800 each;*

2. *Competition was only beginning to develop its own version of the Widget, giving XYZ an approximate two-year lead; and*

3. *The volume of business available to XYZ should allow for a 50 percent profit margin once competition geared up.*

Delivering Value: By Bridging to Actionable Recommendations

A consultant draws his recommendations from conclusions. Conclusions resemble a bridge span. One side of the span rests on the consultant's research: collected data, interview findings, and analysis. The other side supports the consultant's actionable recommendations. Spanning these are the consultant's conclusions. Taken as a whole, these three— research, conclusions, and recommendations— provide a bridge from the client's problem to actionable recommendations.

The answers to three questions guide consultants in building their recommendations: First, what bearing does the data, field interviews, and other findings have on the client's situation? Secondly, toward what client action do the conclusions point? And lastly, how valuable are the consultant's recommendations?

The value added by a consultant's recommendations is judged through the eyes of the client. The client is searching for solutions, for impact on his business or organization, and for ease on implementation. To that end, the consultant's task is to provide the client with maximum value.

Take for example a USA-based manufacturer having significant exports to Brazil. Its Brazilian customers clamor for in-country production and reduced costs. In support of that consideration, the manufacturer asks two separate consultants to answer the identical question: can it obtain a significant cost advantage by manufacturing in Brazil? In performing the assignment, both consultants travel to Brazil. However:

- **Consultant One** interviews the US commercial attaché in Sao Paulo, as well as several freight forwarders and a tax attorney. Based on this work, the consultant calculates at 35% cost advantage.

- **Consultant Two** also holds interviews similar to Consultant One. Additionally, Consultant Two brings client executives into his consulting team. Together, they meet in the USA and in Brazil, with other USA companies with Brazilian manufacturing operations to learn from their experiences. Based on this work, the consultant calculates a 30% cost advantage, and further recommends the client positions itself in the state of Sao Paulo, and joint-ventures with the client's largest distributor. Consultant Two's fee is half again higher than that of Consultant One.

Clearly, the greater value is delivered by Consultant Two. Consultant One identifies a greater cost advantage and did so for a lower fee. Consultant Two however creates greater credibility by involving the client, by delving into existing Brazil operations, and by providing greater specificity relative to implementation.

Returning to Sam Smart's fictional Widget consulting engagement, the example below demonstrates in greater detail, the craft of providing clients with actionable recommendations:

Following completion of interviews, Sam Smart shared his research findings with XYZ's planners. Together, they applied Sam's findings to revising XYZ's initial Widget NPV analysis, as shown below:

	Widget Net Present Value (NPV) Analysis: Revised by Sam Smart							
	Expected Widget Market			XYZ profit margin potential in this Market				
	Units (000)	Price Per unit	Market size ($ mil)	XYZ Market Share	XYZ Sales ($ mil)	Profit Margin %	Profit Margin ($ mil)	Profit Margin NPV @ 9%
Yr 1	25	$800	$20	100%	$20	40%	$8	$8
Yr 2	50	$800	$40	100%	$40	50%	$20	$18
Yr 3	100	$800	$80	75%	$60	50%	$30	$24.3
Yr 4	150	$700	$105	75%	$78.8	40%	$31.5	$23
Yr 5	150	$700	$105	50%	$52.5	40%	$21	$13.8
					Forecast 5-Year NPV of Profit Margin Stream			$85.1

From this, Sam Smart concluded that Widget sales could, over five years, return to XYZ an estimated $85.1million on its $10 million tooling investment. His supporting field interviews confirmed that Widget was needed to defray costs associated with EPA action. XYZ's market entry was timely and well in advance of any competitors.

Sam therefore recommended that XYZ invest in the necessary tooling and begin trials with all three market leaders: Alpha Products, Beta Systems, and Gamma Solutions. XYZ should initially price the product at $800. If XYZ moved well in this *regard, Sam Smart believed, XYZ could pay back its tooling costs within the first two years. Moreover, the program could generate over $80 million in additional gross margin over the next five years*

In this example, the consultant assembled his recommendation by following a systematic approach to his work. The consultant breathed life into his recommendation, using his conclusions to create a bridge to actionable recommendations. By following this proven process, considerable value was added to the client's business.

Delivering Value: By Involving the Client

The client expects to be kept informed; they want to be involved. Consultants satisfy this client need in a variety of ways. The following three client involvements are particularly useful:

- **Progress Meetings** serve a variety of purposes. Early in the engagement, progress meetings are a platform for clarifying the engagement. Later meetings provide the consultants with an opportunity to test their findings. Progress meetings can also explore various ideas for follow-up action. Most important, progress meetings provide both the consultant and client with assurance that their effort will add value to the client.

  Preparation for the progress meetings is no casual undertaking. Some consultants for example prepare by drafting their final report and then using the progress meeting to test the power and relevance of their tentative recommendations. A well-conducted progress meeting may confirm the ongoing path, redirect the engagement, or expand the engagement's scope.

- **Verbal Summaries:** Senior management occasionally requests a brief summary of the consultants' work. The consultant may choose to deliver the summary at the outset of the consultant's final presentation. The consultant may alternatively hold the summary in reserve, anticipating the CEO's request for an impromptu update.

  Either way, the consultant should carefully consider his or her summary. At the least, the consultant should articulate the engagement's governing thought or key question. The consultant should put forward his key recommendation, along with supportive reasoning or controlling evidence. If time allows, the consultant should also present his ideas on implementation. Whatever the message, the consultant should allow for no more than a two-to-three-minute delivery window. Despite its brevity, the verbal summary may prove to be the consultant's most actionable client communication.

- **Delivering the Final Report:** Report preparation begins with the consultant referring back to his or her original proposal, with attention given to the original description of the client's problem or issues. From that base, the typical report leads the client through the consultant's understanding of the situation, any re-defining of the problem, the methodologies employed, key findings, conclusions, and optional courses of action and—finally—recommendations.

Effective client reporting is more than just words, Outlines and graphics. The report's value hinges on its delivery, described here as a three-legged stool. One leg of successful report delivery is format. Report preparers increasingly utilize projection formats, such as Windows' PowerPoint or Mac's Keynote. Consultants of a more traditional bent still rely on written reports that they print and bind. Should the client require extensive data or analytical documentation, the consultant can deliver such information in a variety of formats.

The second leg of the stool is persuasion. Delivering the final report provide consultants with the opportunity to convince client stakeholders to not only accept the consultants' recommendations, but also to decide to act upon the report's recommendations.

The stool's third leg is the final report having its own "legs." By having legs, a final report can successfully be presented by client stakeholders, not just by the consultant. With legs, the report can also be confidently passed along to others in the client organization that lacks an understanding of the consulting engagement's details. Without this leg, the consultant's work could end up being applauded at the final meeting but die as client executives depart the presentation.

Delivering Value: By Making Things Happen

Consultants deliver value by affecting change. The engagement's research and data collection, its interviews, and use of analytical methods provide only part of the consultant's worth. Whether client derives value hinges on what the consultant does with this information. Consultants generate value when they apply the information to guiding clients toward changed behavior.

Persuading clients to implement the consultant's recommendations represents the consultant's final challenge. By themselves, consultants cannot affect change. The decision to change rests with client stakeholders.

Consultants can however shape stakeholder thinking by anticipating issues which, if handled properly, can lead the client toward making the consultant's recommendations a reality. The value of competent consulting rests in shaping the client's tomorrows.

NOTES

Notes in INTRODUCTION

1. Paraphrased from Ben Franklin's Poor Richard's Almanac of November 1743, which reads: "Experience keeps a dear school, yet fools learn in no other."

2. See two works by Ron Alsop: "The Trophy Kids Grow Up: How the Millennial Generation is Shaking Up the Workplace," Jossey-Bass, 2008, and his Wall Street Journal article "The Trophy Kids Go to Work," October 19, 2009.

3. See American Assembly of Collegiate Schools of Business 2002 report: "Management Education at Risk," Page 20, 2002.

4. Two references are provided: W.F. Bynum and R. Porter (Editors) 2005; Oxford Dictionary of Scientific Quotations. Oxford University Press, 2005.

5. See J. Dewey, "Experience and Education," Collier, New York, 1938.

6. See J. Brownell and D.A. Jameson: "Problem-based Learning in Graduate Management Education: an integrative Model and Interdisciplinary Application." Journal of Management Education, 2004.

7. See M.A., Albanese and S. Mitchell: "Problem-based Learning: A Review of the Literature on Outcomes and Implementation Issues," Academic Medicine, volume 68, 1993.

8. Dochy, F. Segers, M. Van den Bossche, P. & Gijbels, D. (2003). "Effects of problem-based learning: A meta-analysis." Learning & Instruction, 13, 533–568.

9. Barrows, H.S. (1996). "Problem-based learning in medicine and beyond." In L. Wilkerson & W.H. Gijselears (Eds.), Bring problem-based learning to higher education: Theory and practice (pp. 3–13). San Francisco: Jossey-Bass.

10. Brownell, J. & Jameson, D.A. (2004). "Problem-based learning in graduate management education: An integrative model and interdisciplinary application." Journal of Management Education, 28, 558–577.

11. Refer to the Brownell and Jameson study, identified above.

12. Several researchers weighed in on this subject. See:

    Albanese, M.A. & Mitchell, S. (1993). "Problem-based learning: A review of the literature on Outcomes and implementation issues." Academic Medicine, 68, 52–81;

    Berkson, L. (1993). "Problem-based learning: Have the expectations been met?" Academic Medicine, 68, 79–88;

Collier, J.A. (2000). "Effectiveness of problem-based curricula: Research and theory." Academic Medicine, 75, 259–266;

Smits, P.B.A., Verbeek, J.H.A.M., & De Buisonje, C.D. (2002). "Problem-based learning in continuing medical education: A review of controlled evaluation studies." British Medical Journal, 321, 153–156;

Vernon, D.T.A. & Blake, R.L. (1993). "Does problem-based learning work? A meta-analysis of evaluative research." Academic Medicine, 68, 550–563;

J.E. Stinson and R.G, Milter (1996) in "Problem-based learning in business education: Curriculum design and implementation issues" (Wilkerson & Gijselears, editors. 1996): Bring problem-based learning to higher education: Theory and practice (pp. 3–13). San Francisco: Jossey-Bass.

13.   See the upcoming 2011 publication by G.M. Smith, Jr. and D. Good, "Upgrading Problem-based Learning by Involving Consulting Professionals", published in Research in Management Consulting Series: Preparing Better Consultants: The Role of Academia, volume 14. 2011.

Revised Notes in section entitled
ROOTS OF MANAGEMENT CONSULTING

1. Information about the referred-to consulting firms was taken from histories as presented on the firms' respective web pages, unless otherwise noted.

2. See Harvard Business School case 9-396-060: "Arthur D Little, Inc.," 1996.

3. See ADL web page, and Harvard Business School case 9-806-035: "McKinsey and globalization of consultancy," 2008.

4. See Harvard Business School case 9-698-027: "Cultivating Capabilities to Innovate: BA&H," 1998.

5. See Harvard Business School case 9-806-035: "McKinsey and Globalization of Consultancy," 2008.

6. See Harvard Business School case 9-402-014: "McKinsey & Co.," 2001.

7. See Harvard case 9-806-035 above.

8. See Harvard case 9-806-035 above.

9. See Harvard Business School case 9-396-060: "Arthur D. Little, Inc.," 1996.

10.   See Harvard case 9-806-035 above.

11.   For greater detail, see Mariam Nafig's "The Fast Track," 1997; also Matthew Rees's article "Mister Powerpoint Goes to Washington," The American Magazine, December 1, 2006.

12.   See careers.deloitte.com.

13.   See Harvard case 9-396-060 above.

14.   See Wikipedia: Boston Consulting Group.

15.   See Wikipedia: Bain and Company.

16.   See Wikipedia: Deloitte Consulting LLP.

17.   See Booz Allen Hamilton report: 1914-2014 Defining Moments.

18.   See Wikipedia: Accenture.

19.   See Harvard Business School case 410112-PDF-ENG: "George Martin at BCG," 2010.

20.   See Harvard Business School case 9-696-096: "Deloitte & Touch Consulting Group," 1996.

21.   The theory of disruptive innovation was first coined by
       Harvard professor Clayton M. Christensen in his research
       on the disk-drive industry and later popularized by his book
       The Innovator's Dilemma, published in 1997.

22.   Gordon Moore, co-founder of Intel, formulated in 1975 that
       the number of electronic components squeezable into a
       single integrated electronic circuit would double every two
       years. His prediction remains a guide in semiconductor
       R&D, and related product development. This phenomenon
       is referred to as Moore's Law.

Notes in WHAT CONSULTANTS DO: INITIATE THE CLIENT
       ENGAGEMENT

1.   More can be learned about Gantt Charts by referring to Peter
       Morris, "The Management of Projects," Thomas Telford,
       1994. Wikipedia has a "Gantt Chart" write-up that is also
       helpful.

2.   More on PERT charts can be found in D.Z. Milosevic's "Pro-
       ject Management Tool Box: Tools and Techniques for the
       Practicing Project Manager." Wiley, 2003. Wikipedia has a
       "PERT Chart" article that is useful.

3.   See Harvard Business School case 0-410-112: "George Martin at BCG," 2010.

4.   See Harvard Business School case 9-396-060: "Arthur D. Little," 1996.

5.   Basis of this diagram is the project management triangle. See the work of Carl S. Chatfield and others, complimenting Microsoft in the application of its Office software.

Notes in WHAT CONSULTANTS DO: APPLY PROBLEM-SOLVING METHODS

1.   Additional information on Best Practices can be found in D.P. Cushman and Sara S. King's "Communicating Best Practices at Dell, General Electric, Microsoft and Monsanto," Suny Press, 2003.

2.   Drawn from the authors' experience.

3.   Additional information on SWOT analysis can be found in E.P. Learned and others' book Business Policy, Text and Cases, Irwin Press, 1969.

4.   More information on hypothesis-driven model can be found in Paul N. Friga's "The McKinsey Engagement," McGraw-Hill, 2008.

5. Application of Hypothesis-Driven Model is further discussed in Ethan Rasiel and Paul Friga's "The McKinsey Way," McGraw-Hill, 1999.

6. More information on Porter's Five-Force Competitive Model can be found in Michael Porter's "The Five Competitive Forces That Shape Strategy," Harvard Business Publishing, 2008.

7. More information on BCG's 2x2 Matrix can be found in Harvard Business School case 9-175-175, "Note on the Boston Consulting Group Concept," 1983.

8. Additional information on DAIMC and Six-Sigma can be found in Geoff Tennant's "SIX SIGMA: SPC and TQM in Manufacturing and Services". Gower Publishing, Ltd. 2001. Wikipedia's write-up is also useful.

9. A more comprehensive description of the Six-Sigma Method is found in Dirk Dusharme's article "Six-Sigma Survey: Breaking Through the Six-Sigma Hype," Quality Digest.

10. See Dirk Dusharme's article above.

11. For additional information on the Pareto Principle, see D.R. Henderson and C.L. Hooper's "Making Great Decisions in Business and Life," Chicago Park Press, 2006.

12. See Henderson and Hooper above.

13. An excellent summary of the application of decision trees is available on Wikipedia under "Decision Tree."

14. For greater detail, see Barbara Minto's "The Minto Pyramid Principle," Minto International, 1996.

15. The failure of corporate acquisitions is well documented. See R.A. Weber and C.F. Camerer's "Cultural Conflict and Merger Failure: An Experimental Approach," Management Science, Volume 49, Number 4, April 2003.

16. More information on the McKinsey 7-S Model can be found in Tom Peters and R.H. Waterman's "In Search of Excellence," Harper Business Essentials, 2004.

17. See P. Ghemawat's article "Building Strategy on the Experience Curve," Harvard Business Review, March–April 1985.

18. Scenario planning is further described in "Scenario Planning", Darden Business Publishing, University of Virginia. UV0842, 2007.

19. For more extensive discussion, see David Garvin and Lynne Levesque's article: "A Note on Scenario Planning," Harvard Business School, 2006. Also, see Paul Schoemaker and Cornelius van der Heijden's "Integrating Scenarios into Strategic Planning at Royal Dutch/Shell," Planning Review, Vol. 20(3): 1992, pp. 41–46.

20. Wikipedia further describes Net Present Value on "Net Present Value."

21. Wikipedia further describes Ishikawa or Fishbone diagrams on "Ishikawa Diagram."

22. The application of Logic Trees is further described in Ken Watanabe's "Problem Solving 101," Portfolio, the Penguin Group, 2009.

23. Wikipedia provides a summary description of Value Chain analysis. For greater detail, go to Michael Porter's "Competitive Advantage: Creating and Sustaining Superior Performance," Harvard Publishing, 1985.

24. Game Theory is further described in R.M. Grant's "Contemporary Strategic Analysis," Edition six, pp. 99–105, Blackwell Publishing, 2008.

25. See Gerald Katz's "The Voice of the Customer. The PDMA Tool book for New Product Development," 2004. John Wiley & Sons.

26. See Abraham Maslow's "Motivation and Personality," 1945, Harper and Row Publishers.

APPENDICES

Appendix A: Blazing Saddles example: PERT Schedule

Appendix B: Blazing Saddles example: Proposed Fee Build-up

Appendix C: Blazing Saddles example: Engagement Proposal

Appendix D: Consulting Engagement Plan: Template

Appendix E: Consulting Engagement Plan: Example

Appendix A: Blazing Saddles example: PERT Schedule

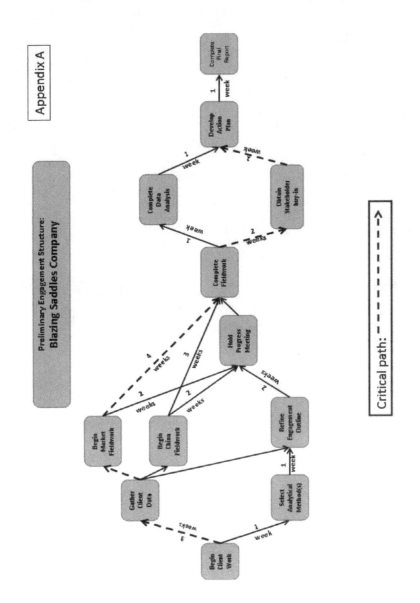

Confidential to Smart Consultants, Inc.

Staffing Plan
Blazing Saddles Company

1) Intended Consulting Staff & billing rates:
Sam Smart, managing partner: $300 per hour.
Jennifer Jackson, engagement manager: $200 per hour.
Ben Woodbridge, consultant (generalist): $125 per hour.
George Hsu, contacted supply chain consultant (Taiwan-based): $400 per hour.

2) Hours estimated to complete the engagement:

Engagement Tasks (based on PERT Engagement Outline)	By Sam Smart	By engagement manager Jennifer Jackson	By consultant Ben Woodbridge	By contractor George Hsu
Begin Client Work	4 hours	24 hours	16 hours	
Gather Client Data			120	
Perform Market Fieldwork - before Progress Meeting			160	40 hours
Perform China Fieldwork - before Progress Meeting	4	8	40	
Select appropriate analytical method(s) & refine the engagement plan.		16	40	
Hold Progress Meeting	8	16	40	
Sub-total: hours through Progress Meeting	**16 hours**	**64 hours**	**416 hours**	**40 hours**
Perform Market Fieldwork - after Progress Meeting				40
Perform China Fieldwork - after Progress Meeting			40	
Complete Data Analyses	8	16	80	
Obtain Stakeholder Buy-In	8	16	40	
Develop Action Plan & Complete Final Report	8	16	40	
Final Presentation to client				
Total hours	**40 hours**	**128 hours**	**616 hours**	**80 hours**

3) Estimated consultants' costs at their hourly rate:

Thru progress meeting:	$4,800	$12,800	$52,000	$16,000
Total	$12,000	$25,600	$77,000	$32,000

4) Fee Calculation (before expenses):

	Thru progress meeting	Total
Total Consultants' Cost:	$85,600	$146,600
Fee calculation: at 2x markup	$171,200	$293,200
With contingency	$175,000	$300,000

161

Appendix C: Blazing Saddles example: Engagement Proposal

Smart Consultants, Inc.
222 Keystone Way
Pittsburgh, Pennsylvania 15222

January 1, 2012

Ms. Donna Blazer
President and Chief Executive Officer
Blazing Saddles Company
Pittsburgh, Pennsylvania

Subject: Proposal for a Consulting Engagement

Dear Ms. Blazer,

We appreciate this opportunity to assist Blazing Saddles. Following our recent meeting, we at Smart Consultants developed the engagement proposal below. Please consider.

Our Understanding of Your Situation.

Blazing Saddles has over the past five years positioned itself as a major supplier to the global horse competition industry, selling high-end leather products to race tracks, rodeo performers, foxhunt enthusiasts, and competitive horse showers of all sorts. Its products include saddles, bridles and leather clothing.

Blazing Saddles obtains it leather and performs partial assembly from a Shanghai leather processor. Custom engraving, finishing and packaging is performed in the company's Pittsburgh facility. Blazing Saddles distributes worldwide, having constructed a network of retail saddle shops and professional distributors. Company sales reached $100 million two years ago, but has since experienced deteriorating profits.

You feel that action must immediately be taken. You believe that product cost is one source of the problem. More recently however, you determined that competitor Horses-R-Us promotes its leather products as American made and suggests that you are Asian-owned.

You are therefore in need of answers to two questions. First, how can Blazing Saddles counter Horses-R-Us' negative advertising? Secondly, are there any significant opportunities for cost improvement, in your supply chain?

Our Approach to the Engagement.

We are prepared to answers these questions, and others that may arise during the engagement. In doing so, we will provide Blazing Saddles with an actionable program designed to return the company to sales and profit growth. To do so, we intend to proceed as follows:

- **Scope:** We will proceed down two parallel paths. First, we will determine the strengths and weaknesses of your competitor's products and marketing strategy. Secondly, we will identify and assess your product's major cost components, from China through Pittsburgh final assembly and on to retail shelves.

- **Intended Work:** The assigned Smart consultants will begin by studying your internal cost data, and assessing your sales and profitability from a product and sales channel perspective. Thereafter, we will conduct a range of field interviews, focusing on individuals knowledgeable in both your supply chain (including your Chinese supplier) and product distribution (selected distributors, retailers, and customers). We will also attend key industry trade shows scheduled over the next few months.

- **Deliverables:** Two deliverables are key: a comprehensive cost assessment of each critical step in your supply chain, and results of market interviews. From these two deliverables, I and my engagement manager will deliberate with your senior staff, to develop options, frame a program, and lay out a near-term action plan.

  By about the fifth week, we will be prepared to review our findings, and tentative conclusions. Thereafter, additional field work may be required to sharpen our assessment. The final weeks of this 12-week assignment will be devoted to discussions between ourselves and your staff, to refine your options and develop a meaningful action program.

- **Assistance asked of Blazing Saddles:** At the outset of the engagement, we will need sales records covering the past several years. We also will need cost and performance data covering your entire supply chain. For the market-related work, we wish to interview your sales management and, thereafter, have access to selected retailers and distributors. Give the critical nature of this engagement and the need for rapid action, please assign a senior marketing executive to work with us, to be part of our team.

- **Engaged Consultants:** We will assemble a team of appropriately experienced consultants. I will of course organize the engagement, and participate downstream as we develop options and recommendations. We will also assign Jennifer Jackson as engagement manager, responsible for conducting the assignment. Ms. Jackson brings ten years of experience to this engagement. She is particularly qualified in performing competitive assessments in a retail space. She will be part-time on the assignment.

  Two consultants will be assigned. One will focus on the USA portion of your issue, focusing on supply chain and competitive assessment. Additionally, a China outsourcing expert will join our team.

<u>Timetable and Fee</u>: Given your approval, we are prepared to begin work within two weeks. The engagement would be completed in three months. To proceed, we ask your approval of our $300,000 fee, with 50% paid at outset and the remainder paid upon completion. Travel and related expenses will be invoiced separately, with overseas travel authorized in advance.

We hope you find this proposal acceptable, and look forward to working with Blazing Saddles.

Regards,

Sam Smart
Managing Partner

Appendix D: Consulting Engagement Plan: Template

CONSULTING
ENGAGEMENT PLAN

CLIENT: _____

CONSULTING TEAM: _____

TEAM ADVISOR: _____

The signatures below indicate that this Engagement Plan is agreed to by the Client, Consulting Team, and Team Advisor

_____ _____ _____
Signature of Client   *Consultant*   *Consultant*
Representative   *Signature*   *Signature*

_____ _____ _____
Name and Title   *Consultant*   *Consultant*
                          Signature   *Signature*

_____
Date   *Signature of Team Advisor*

SECTION 1   DESCRIPTION OF THE CONSULTING ENGAGEMENT

A. Understanding of Relevant Client History:

B. Description of the Client's Problem or Issue:

C. Understanding of the Client's Desires and Expectations:

- The specific engagement objective:

- A suitable measurement or validation of success:

- The client's desired timetable for success:

D. How the Team Intends to Proceed:

- Scope of Work:

- Intended methods and/or analytical framework:

SECTION 2: ENGAGEMENT SCHEDULE AND TASKS

Tasks & Events:	Week ending:																
Hold Client kickoff meeting																	
Gain Work Plan Signoff.																	
#1:																	
#2:																	
Hold mid-project client review (indicate date & time)																	
#3:																	
#4:																	
Make final presentation (indicate date & time)																	

Task #1 description:	Task #2 description:
Task #3 description:	Task #4 description:
Additional Task:	Additional Task:

169

SECTION 3   INFORMATION REQUIRED FROM THE CLIENT

SECTION 4   KEY CONTACT INFORMATION

Position	Name	Address	Telephone #	Fax #	E-mail address
Lead Client Executive					
Other Executive(s)					
Team Member					
Team Member					
Team Member					
Team Member					
Team Lead					
Team Advisor					

SECTION 5   ENGAGEMENT BUDGET

Category	Description	Estimated $ Amount
Local Travel		
Out-of-area Travel		
Other		
Total Budget:		

170

Appendix E: Consulting Engagement Plan: Example

Example

CONSULTING ENGAGEMENT PLAN

Example

CLIENT: _____BeWitch.com_____

CONSULTING TEAM: Joe Smith   Jane Doe   Jim Brown   Charles Murphy   Karen Jones

TEAM ADVISOR: Elizabeth Reed

The signatures below indicate that this Engagement Plan is agreed to by the Client, Consulting Team, and Team Advisor

Judy Schulz   *Joe Smith*   *Jane Doe*   *Jim Brown*

| Signature of Client Representative | Consultant Signature | Consultant Signature | Consultant Signature |

Judy Schulz, Marketing Director   *Charles Murphy*   *Karen Jones*   *Elizabeth Reed*

| Name and Title | Consultant Signature | Consultant Signature | Consultant Signature |

September 1

Date   Signature of Team Advisor

171

SECTION 1 DESCRIPTION OF THE CONSULTING ENGAGEMENT

A. Understanding of Relevant Client History:

BeWitch.com is the global leader in online book sales, having created the business several years ago. BeWitch.com maintained strong double-digit sales growth in its early years while innovating one-click shopping check-out, and by expanding into consumer electronics. In recent years however, the company's sales growth flattened. Currently, BeWitch.com is currently operating at a loss.

B. Description of the Client's Problem or Issue:

BeWitch.com believes that growth can be achieved by entering the more sophisticated business-to-business e-commerce market. Given it precarious financial situation, BeWitch.com further believes that it can expand if it leverages its organizational and financial strengths while avoiding unexpected pitfalls in entering a new market.

C. Understanding of the Client's Desires and Expectations:

- **The specific engagement objective:** *Identify three attractive e-commerce markets where no clear competitor dominates.*

- **A suitable measurement or validation of success:** *BeWitch.com expects its MBA team to:*
  - *provide convincing evidence that each of the three markets have a $100 million revenue potential for the company, and*
  - *gain support of BeWitch.com's executive committee to this undertaking.*

- **The client's desired timetable for success:** *The client should be in the three markets within 18 months.*

D. How the Team Intends to Proceed:

- **Scope of Work:** *The team will initially assess through interviews, the client's e-commerce capabilities and intended strategy. Thereafter, the team will travel to Houston, attending the industry's National e-Commerce Expo, during which team members will assess market needs and the competitive environment through interviewers with customers, suppliers and market influencers. Following a mid-term client progress meeting, they will assess the client's intended e-commerce platform and develop recommendations.*

- **Intended methods and/or analytical framework:** *Perform a SWOT analysis as basis for develop the client's value chain. Thereafter, create and test various market opportunities using a 2x2 matrix as a descriptive tool.*

172

SECTION 2: ENGAGEMENT SCHEDULE AND TASKS

Tasks & Events: / Week ending:	9/7	9/14	9/21	9/28	10/5	10/12	10/19	10/26	11/2	11/9	11/16	11/23	11/30	12/2	12/9	12/19
Hold Client kickoff meeting	■															
Gain Work Plan Signoff.		■														
#1: Assess the client's e-commerce capability.		■	■													
#2: Study market needs & attend e-Expo convention.				■	■	■	■	■	■							
Hold mid-project client review (indicate date & time)							Oct 17 @ 4 pm →									
#3: Study the client's intended e-comm platforms.											■	■	■			
#4: Assess options & develop recommendations.												■	■	■		
Make final presentation (indicate date & time)															←	Dec 19 @ 4 pm

Task #1 description: Assess client's e- commerce capability.
- Conduct Internal/external stakeholder interviews.
- Map the client's SWOT and value chain.
- Construct initial hypotheses on direction of strategy.

Task #3 description: Assess the intended e-comm platform.
- Review intended concepts with client stakeholders.
- Rank potential markets using Pareto Analysis and DC.
- Develop a detailed risks and opportunities analysis.

Additional Task: None

Task #2 description: Study needs & competitive situation; attend annual e-Expo Convention in Houston.
- Complete travel logistics and develop interview plan.
- Two team members attend, hold interviews, and summarize.
- Team develops conclusions and tentative recommendations.

Task #4 description: Finalize team recommendations.
- Develop revenue forecast and required client support.
- Test recommendation via client discussions.
- Complete final report in both text and PowerPoint formats.

Additional Task:

SECTION 3 INFORMATION REQUIRED FROM THE CLIENT

1. *Provide team with a copy of independent consultant's 2009 e-commerce report, and related client documents.*
2. *Identify knowledgeable non-client individuals expected to attend national e-Expo convention.*

SECTION 4 KEY CONTACT INFORMATION

Position	Name	Address	Telephone #	Fax #	E-mail address
Lead Client Executive	Judy Schulz, Director	235 Fifth Ave, Pittsburgh	412- 123-4577	412-123-5678	judys@BeWitch.com
Other Executive(s)	Jeff Bench, President		412-123-4568	412-123-5678	jeffb@BeWitch.com
Team Member	Charles Murphy		412-987-6521	412-875-5432	chasmurphy@acme.com
Team Member	Jane Doe	Acme Consultants, Liberty Towers 100 Liberty Avenue, Pittsburgh, PA	412-987-6522	412-875-5432	janedoe@acme.com
Team Member	Joe Smith		412-987-6523	412-875-5432	joesmith@acme.com
Team Member	Jim Brown		412-987-6524	412-875-5432	jimbrown@acme.com
Team Lead	Karen Jones		412-987-6525	412-875-5432	karenjones@acme.com
Team Advisor	Elizabeth Reed		412-987-6543	412-987-6542	elizreed@acme.com

SECTION 5 ENGAGEMENT BUDGET

Category	Description	Estimated $ Amount
Local Travel	Car usage at $0.50 per mile	$175.00
Out-of-area Travel	Air, Hotel, Meals (two to Houston)	$2,000.00
Other	Printing and binding of final report	$125.00
Total Budget:		$2,300.00